<California Local Agency Formation Commissions>

RICHARD T. LEGATES

National Housing and
Development Law Project
Earl Warren Legal Institute
School of Law

171756

INSTITUTE OF GOVERNMENTAL STUDIES
UNIVERSITY OF CALIFORNIA, BERKELEY

1970

$2.75

International Standard Book Number (ISBN) 0-87772-066-5
Library of Congress Catalog Card Number 71-629190

CONTENTS

TABLES

vii

APPENDICES

PREFACE

The purpose of this monograph is to present a suc-
cinct and balanced description of California's Local
Agency Formation Commissions. The paper combines an examination of the way the commissions came into being,
with discussions of their current operations and possibilities for the future. The presentation, however, is
purposely asymmetrical in that major attention is devoted to more recent developments that have not been described elsewhere.

Further, a major thesis is that LAFCos are developing into planning entities, and for that reason a dis-
proportionate amount of space is devoted to a documenta-
tion of planning developments. Finally, I have limited
my study and discussion to the operations of LAFCos in
the urban counties of California. While there are LAFCos
in 57 California counties (the exception being the City
and County of San Francisco), the preponderance of activity and innovative ideas is concentrated in the dozen
or so most populous counties.

I have addressed this monograph to a diverse reader-
ship. Students of local government in California and in
other states, who are following the LAFCo innovation,
should find the chapters describing LAFCo operations
pertinent. While much of this material will be familiar
to those more intimately involved in the operations of
LAFCos, they too may find something useful in the legislative history of the commissions, the experience of
other states, and the aggregate figures on state activity.

This inquiry was made possible by support from the
Institute of Governmental Studies at the University of
California at Berkeley. I am indebted to Professor

Eugene C. Lee and Stanley Scott of the Institute for their direction of my work. I am also grateful to Dean William L. C. Wheaton of the College of Environmental Design and Professor Lawrence Sullivan of the School of Law, both at Berkeley; Professor John C. Bollens of the University of California, Los Angeles; Robert B. Rigney, executive officer of the San Bernardino LAFCo; Peggy L. McElligott of the law firm of Wilson, Jones, Morton and Lynch; and William Zion, consultant to the Intergovern- mental Council on Urban Growth in their LAFCo study, for their vigorous critiques of drafts of the monograph.

The bulk of the research for this study was carried out between January 1 and June 1, 1968. Some more re- cent developments were inserted prior to publication, but the manuscript does not purport to cover fully de- velopments subsequent to June 1, 1968.

Richard T. LeGates

The Formation of Local Governmental Agencies: Problems and Alternative Solutions

This chapter explores the conditions in California that led to the creation of Local Agency Formation Commissions in 1963, and traces the development of the legislation that established them. The chapter's first section describes the anarchic situation with respect to changes in city boundaries, incorporation of new cities, and formation of special districts. The next section explains the way in which other states have attempted to deal with these types of problems. Our attention then turns to the political and legislative history of the California LAFCo legislation and an examination of the unique characteristics of LAFCos.

Such a study of LAFCos is by no means merely an academic or antiquarian exercise. In fact, LAFCos are such new institutions that future modification of their powers is almost inevitable. In order to forecast and guide their evolution, it may also be instructive to examine the experiences (good and bad) of other states as well.

2

THE SITUATION BEFORE THE CREATION OF LAFCOS

There is little need to document the phenomenal growth of California's population in past decades, but it is important to observe where most of this population has chosen to reside. The most recent comprehensive statistical survey of population location in the state found that:

> [From 1950-1960] The overall growth rate of urban fringe areas was 112%, an average annual increase of 11%. Central cities of metropolitan areas accounted for only about one-fifth of the State's total population increase for the decade, and only increased at an annual average rate of 2.6%.[1]

It is also significant that the growth rate in nonmetropolitan areas was 33 percent in this 10 year period. In the interest of orderly growth and the rational provision of urban services, the major type of change in governmental structure in the state should have been constant annexation of fringe lands to existing cities. California's annexation statutes, however, are antiquated and cumbersome, requiring the approval of a majority of voters in any area proposed for annexation. Annexation therefore tended to occur most often in two kinds of areas: (1) uninhabited territory, and (2) land that had a particularly valuable tax base. (See Ch. III, section on "Eliminating Raids on the Tax Base.")

To take away a parcel of land containing the major tax base from an area, by means of incorporation, is frequently unfair to the residents and governmental agencies in the surrounding unincorporated area. Furthermore, competition for annexation has often forced cities to lower subdivision standards so as to include land with "deals" that proved disastrous in the long run. In the rapidly urbanizing areas, particularly in

Santa Clara County, border problems were a source of
constant conflict and occasional litigation between
cities.

Because annexation is relatively difficult in
California, the alternative choice of incorporation
or the formation of a new city has some attractive
features. The California incorporation statute is extremely permissive. The only requirement concerning
the nature of an area to be incorporated is that there
be at least 500 inhabitants within the community. In
Los Angeles County, however, the requirement calls for
500 voters.[2] Because of the laxity of requirements
prior to 1963, many cities were incorporated "defen-
sively" to prevent annexation by other contiguous
cities, or to seal off areas as tax shelters.

Meanwhile, a complex web of special districts
grew up to provide services in many areas that were
left out of the pattern of annexation and incorporation.
These entities are authorized by California's voluminous,
complex special district laws, that make the formation
of most types of districts relatively easy. Because
districts may be tailor-made for one purpose, they are
attractive to those who prefer to deal with governmental
problems incrementally. As a consequence, the number
of special districts has grown enormously since World
War II. Without a watchdog supervisory agency, they
have been directed towards many parochial ends destruc-
tive of orderly and rational growth.

Thus the difficulties and the competition involved
in annexation, combined with the relative ease of incorporation and district formation, together produced a
jumble of local government forms in California. Before
the LAFCos, annexation, incorporation, and district
formation all demonstrated distinctive weaknesses that
called for regulation.

City Annexations

One has only to look at a map showing the border contours of California cities to recognize some of the problems posed by lack of control over city annexations. "Strips" extend several miles along highways; "cherry stems" reach along roads and circle around shopping centers; and "corridors" of undesirable land remain between cities. Cities are doughnut-shaped or pockmarked, or contrived in shapes too fanciful and too complex to describe.

The classic example is the City of San Jose, which has lacy fingers stretching out like those of a sea anemone in all directions. In the decade before the LAFCo came into existence, San Jose annexed 685 discrete parcels of land.[3] Many of these boundaries present problems, because they describe areas that are costly, difficult, and inefficient to service.

Incorporations

Lack of regulation permits two sorts of undesirable consequences: the "special interest" and the "defensive" incorporation. Many special interest cities have provided tax benefits for their inhabitants and posed financial problems for their neighbors. Industry, California, which was incorporated in 1957 in Los Angeles County, is a classic example. It has 20 dwelling units per square mile. If the unit figure is multiplied by 2.6, the median occupation rate per dwelling unit in Los Angeles County (as noted in the 1960 census), Industry's population density would be approximately 52 per square mile as compared with 5,127 per square mile, the average density for cities in Los Angeles County. Industry's per capita assessed valuation is $54,868, compared with $2,183 for the county as a whole. As one author wrote:

> The City of Industry represents the
> most specialized use of municipal
> authority to create an industrial

enclave in the post-1950 cities. A
threat of the possible annexation
of prime industrial territory and
the availability of sales tax revenue were important factors in
the decision of property owners
to seek incorporation. The chairman of the incorporation committee
pointed out that the proposed city
would be composed of over 90 percent commercial and industrial
property and that, while his group
was more than satisfied with
existing county services: "Our
sole aim is to attract additional
industry, and it is hoped that we
can maintain complete freedom
from the tax burdens which con-
front other cities. With the
creation of this new industrial
entity, we hope that in due time
we can reduce extensively, if
not entirely the personal property tax."[4]

Clearly, such a "tax shelter" city, low in population and high in assessed valuation, can afford a low
tax rate. Receipts from property and sales taxes can
be plowed into facilities designed to serve industry.
Thus the location of industrial enterprises is determined by artificial inducements, rather than by more
rational factors such as favorable topography, access
to transportation, and availability of a suitable work
force.

Industry is only one example of an "industrial"
city; Vernon and Commerce are two other prime examples
in Los Angeles County. But the term "industrial" is
too narrow to characterize the special interests that
may be served by such cities. Dairyland protects the
interests of dairymen, Irwindale defends a rock and

gravel quarry, and the very rich are sheltered by
Rolling Hills Estates. Of 26 new cities incorporated
in Los Angeles County during a seven-year period in
the 1950's, more than one-third were special interest
incorporations.[5]

Before 1963, another major abuse of the incorporation statute was the purely "defensive" incorporation.
Frequently, a group of citizens in an area contiguous
to an expanding city would incorporate solely in order
to avoid the possibility of being annexed. A recent
survey of 47 cities incorporated between 1950 and 1963
in California, revealed that 14 listed "against annexation" as a major motive for incorporation.[6]

Special Districts

Special district government in the United States
has been under heavy attack during the last decade.
There are persuasive arguments that government by
many small districts is both inefficient and undemocratic. The California State Assembly Committee on
Municipal and County Government has found that:

> ...local autonomy does not always pro-
> vide the grassroots control it is pre-
> sumed to, since district government
> tends to be confusing to the citizen.
> The citizen is often at a loss to know
> where to go to register a complaint,
> which district is providing what ser-
> vice, and what the tax dollar is being
> spent for. In order to be a conscien-
> tious citizen, residents of some areas
> would have to keep up with the activi-
> ties of as many as 10 or 12 governments.
> Poor district voting records indicate
> that the average citizen has little
> interest in the day-to-day activities

of districts, probably due to the
large number and their small-scale
operations.[7]

The report observes that lack of public knowledge in
the special district field is shown by the 10 percent
average turnout at district elections.[8]

In the absence of regulation or supervision, many
districts were formed for the benefit of a few developers or limited special interests. They offered
little if any benefits to the general public, and sometimes quite the opposite.[9]

Of even greater significance is the fact that without some coordination in their operations, districts
provide shortsighted and inefficient government. Professor John Bollens of the University of California at
Los Angeles, in writing of "urban fringe" districts,
made the following pungent observations, which are in
some measure applicable to all special district government:

> Several overlapping urban fringe dis-
> tricts in an area usually constitute a
> web of small, costly operations, lack-
> ing adequate land-use and regulatory
> authority as well as recognizable
> boundaries. Many fringe residents
> argue erroneously that the condition
> of their area is solely their own
> business or concern. What is par-
> ticularly ironic is their frequent
> failure to realize that the gradual
> accretion of special districts even-
> tually results in uneconomic govern-
> ment....
>
> Limited purpose urban fringe dis-
> tricts are uneconomic in another way
> that has more far-reaching effects.
> Emphasizing one service without

coordinating it with others and without exercising needed regulation and
controls, they foster poor fringe
development which is expensive to
undo in the future. They are also
criticized for splintering governmental functions into so many partially overlapping compartments
that the individual district, un-
observed and unnoticed by the public,
may become irresponsive and irrespon-
sible.[10]

By 1963, conditions in California had become so
anarchic that they were intolerable. The pressures of
the population boom and the speed of urbanization were
forcing continuous modifications in governmental structure throughout the state. Laws designed for a simpler
era were not effective in controlling the avarice and
myopia of contending entities. Various pressures were
creating an unmanageable and inequitable patchwork of
governments unresponsive to the needs of the people of
California.

SOLUTIONS PROPOSED BY OTHER STATES

Before focusing on the proposals that received the
most serious attention in California, and examining the
lineup of contending interest groups in the state, a
look at solutions found by other states may help to put
the California debate in perspective. The examples of
Alaska, Texas, and Virginia, which took widely diver-
gent approaches to regulation of city boundary changes,
suggest the spectrum of alternatives.

Texas

Texas exercises even less control over municipal
boundary changes than California did prior to the establishment of LAFCos. Article XI, s. 5 of the Texas State

Constitution vests strong "home rule" powers in all
Texas cities with populations of more than 5,000. Among
the powers a home rule charter may confer upon a municipality, Article 1175 of the implementing legislation
expressly includes

> power to fix the boundary limits of
> any said city, to provide for the
> extension of said boundary limits
> and the annexation of additional
> territory lying adjacent to said
> city, according to such rules as
> may be provided by said charter.[11]

In essence, a city in Texas has the power to annex
land unilaterally without the consent of residents of
the outlying area, so long as the city charter contains
a provision authorizing the city to do so. The Texas
Municipal Annexations Act does provide minimal pro-
cedural and substantive limitations on this power.

The act requires that land annexed must be contiguous to the city, must not be within the territo-
rial jurisdiction of another city, and must be within
the "extraterritorial jurisdiction" of the annexing
city. The latter is determined by the size of the
city's population. For example, a population of 25,000
to 50,000 provides extraterritorial jurisdiction over
all contiguous unincorporated land within two miles
of the city limits.

In addition, for annexation: (1) A public hearing is required. (2) Within one calendar year, a city
may add an area no larger than 10 percent of its
total corporate area as of the first day of that calendar year, with the following exception. If the city
does not take in the full amount authorized in any
year(s), the remainder may be carried and used in
subsequent calendar years, although a city may never
take in an area that is equal to more than 30 percent of its size in any given year. (3) In some
instances, when a home rule city annexes territory,

it must have the consent of those in the area proposed for annexation. (4) If the city fails to provide
governmental and proprietary services within three years
after annexation, residents of the area may petition
for deannexation.[12]

Some charter cities provide for unilateral annexation based on elections within the city. More than 50
cities have charter provisions that allow residents (of
the area to be annexed) to express consent by petition
or election. At least 75 cities have charters that
provide for unilateral annexation by act of the city's
governing body. An example of this type of charter
provision is that of the City of Austin:

> The City Council shall have power by
> ordinance to fix the boundary limits
> of the City of Austin; and to provide
> for the alteration and extension of
> said boundary limits, and the annexa-
> tion of additional territory lying
> adjacent to the city, with or with-
> out the consent of the territory and
> the inhabitants annexed;...when any
> additional territory has been so
> annexed, same shall be a part of the
> City of Austin, and the property
> situated therein shall bear its pro
> rata part of the taxes levied by the
> City, and the inhabitants thereof
> shall be entitled to all the rights
> and privileges of all the citizens,
> and shall be bound by the acts,
> ordinances, resolutions, and regula-
> tions of the city.[13]

Not even the most vigorous proponents of California's municipal home rule wanted to follow the
Texas model of unilateral annexation. Distaste for
the Texas pattern rested on its failure to require
the consent of those annexed, relate controls to
rationality, or inquire into motives.

Alaska

In striking contrast to Texas, the State of Alaska vests strong control over annexation in a state level board, with parallel provisions allowing boundary changes by popular determination. The Alaska Boundary Commission, appointed by the governor, is located within the state local affairs agency.[14] Its five members are appointed for five-year overlapping terms, and include one person from each of the four major state senatorial districts and one from the state at large. The commission is empowered to conduct meetings and hearings, to consider local government boundary changes, and to present proposals for those changes to the legislature. While in theory the commission has only the power to propose, in practice, its powers are important. To nullify a commission proposal, the legislature must enact a resolution concurred in by a majority of the members of each house within 45 days after the proposal is presented, or at the end of the session, whichever is earlier. Otherwise, commission proposals automatically become effective.

As originally proposed, the California LAFCo legislation would have created a state level review board, and there was ample discussion of such a board during the LAFCo hearings. Powers as strong as those of the Alaska board were not, however, seriously advocated. The concept of a state-level board with absolute power to make decisions affecting local government entities without their approval or veto, offended the powerful home rule forces in California.

Virginia

Virginia is notable among the states in that it vests in the judiciary the power to decide boundary questions.[15] During the California LAFCo debate, argument was never seriously focused on this approach. In Virginia, a three judge "annexation court" is impaneled

to hear annexation cases. One judge comes from the
county concerned, and two are brought in from other
counties. Each court convenes on an ad hoc basis to
hear a single case.

Proceedings take the form of trials with arguments
by counsel, and all the paraphernalia of judicial proceedings. The advantages of such a system include the
assurance of impartiality (freedom from political influence), and completeness in the presentation of evidence
by counsel. The disadvantages include the fact that a
court is ill-equipped for the technical fact-finding
that would be suitable for an administrative tribunal.
In Virginia, because the court serves on an ad hoc
basis, it does not accumulate data and expertise in
this specialized field. (One could, however, envision
a court organized to avoid such disadvantages.) Further, court procedures are likely to be slow and costly,
involving formalities of pleading and technical rules
of evidence. In California, experience has shown that
most proposals coming before LAFCos do not require elaborate presentations, although some LAFCos have found a
"swearing-in" procedure helpful in obtaining objective
testimony.

CALIFORNIA FINDS A FORMULA

In California, the debate about regulation covered
a range of alternatives narrower than those explored by
other states. Discussions ranged from only minor modifications of the existing system to the creation of a
state board with power to initiate proposals (which
would be subject to approval by voters or by municipal
bodies). Modifications toward less regulation (as in
Texas), or more (as in Alaska), were discarded after the
initial study; and the possibility of entrusting supervision of boundary changes, incorporations, and special
district formations to the judiciary failed to win serious consideration.

Within the narrowed range of choices, debate crystallized around the proposals of four influential groups: the Governor's Commission on Metropolitan Area Problems, the County Supervisors Association of California, the League of California Cities, and the office of the State Attorney General. Through a series of hearings, and the negotiation of political compromises, the Assembly Interim Committee on Municipal and County Government under the leadership of Assemblyman John T. Knox prepared the statute for legislative passage.

In its final form, the LAFCo law provided for bringing together a number of review functions: for example those concerning annexation, incorporation, and special district problems. Such responsibilities might logically have been entrusted to separate regulatory bodies, since at various times reform groups have focused on only one or two of these functions. The LAFCo formula, however, perceived the various review functions as merely different aspects of a single problem.

The 1955 Report

The first comprehensive review of state annexation policy was conducted in 1955, when Assemblyman Clark Bradley was chairman of the Assembly Interim Committee on Municipal and County Government.[16] Although the committee found numerous problems in the state at that time, it suggested only minor corrective legislation. The final report summarized hearings conducted in rapidly urbanizing Santa Clara County in the following words:

> Extreme competition exists between cities for this fast developing valley area...[we have found] numerous and extended use of strip annexation...numerous lawsuits between cities over disputed annexations...the lowering of present

> county subdivision lot sizes, road
> width and drainage standards by a
> city to encourage annexation to a
> particular city...[and that] pseudo
> islands are being created through
> use of strips or otherwise by
> leaving narrow corridors of unin-
> corporated territory to link the
> surrounded unincorporated terri-
> tory with the outside....

Despite this and much other evidence of a troublesome
legal situation, the committee decided that nothing
need be done. Its report stated:

> The committee concludes that the
> present annexation procedures...
> are essentially a workable and
> fairly equitable means of adding
> territory to an incorporated
> community...active and complete
> cooperation between all local
> governmental agencies on a
> voluntary basis is absolutely
> essential....[17] [Emphasis
> added]

Thus, with explicit findings that existing annexation laws were not workable and equitable, but with a
stated conclusion that they were, the committee in 1955
put the lid back on the annexation problem and let it
simmer for another half decade. Throughout the 1950's
a series of remedial measures chipped away at the worst
problems; in fact, more than 20 amendments to the
Annexation Section of the *Government Code* were passed
between 1949 and 1959. The volume and complexity of
reform legislation contributed to the growing conviction
that a full-scale assault on the jungle was necessary.

Parallel to the hearings on annexation problems, the assembly committee continued a series of investigations of special district government in California, with repeated findings of conflict and inefficiency, and scattered findings of flagrant corruption.[18] By 1960, the committee had begun a second round of hearings and analyses, which culminated in the LAFCo statute. The committee's reports included proposals made by diverse groups in which pressures for reform had apparently developed simultaneously.[19]

The County Supervisors' Position

Of the four major groups noted earlier, the County Supervisors Association of California (hereafter CSAC), took the position that deviated least from the status quo. The heart of their proposal was to create a new state agency with purely advisory powers, with jurisdiction over annexation, incorporation, and boundary changes of autonomous special districts, but without authority even to submit advisory opinions on special districts that were governed by county boards of supervisors.

The CSAC position was based on two earlier association policy statements: "Principles of County Home Rule," (1957) and "Metropolitan Area Principles for Counties," (1959). Both favored the continuation of strong county home rule, and the handling of the "metropolitan area problem" by multifunctional special districts controlled by county supervisors. Thus the CSAC saw the proposed state commission as a purely "technical" fact-gathering entity with no real power.

The CSAC proposed various reforms for streamlining and cleaning up the tangle of annexation and special district laws. Their reform ideas were shared by most groups that testified before the assembly committee.

Attitude of the League of California Cities

Perhaps the most articulate and comprehensive summary of reform suggestions was that made by Lewis Keller, the associate counsel for the League of California Cities, in his presentation to the committee. When Keller made his statement, the league had not finally decided upon its policy. Consequently, Keller suggested a variety of remedial measures, and as one alternative tentatively suggested creation of a state-level review board performing LAFCo-type functions. As the hearings developed, the league's divided views provided a bridge between the CSAC's position on weak controls and the Governor's Commission's proposal, favoring strong controls. Most of the league proposals for modification of legislation remain valid today.

The league suggested first, that cities be permitted to conduct summary annexation of islands, strips, and corridors of unincorporated land if they demonstrated that such areas could be more economically served through annexation. Approval by the county board of supervisors would be required. Second, cities should be allowed to initiate annexation procedures to take inhabited (as well as uninhabited) areas. The league also proposed legislation to promote enforceable intercity annexation agreements, to permit annexations across county lines, and to provide limited city services to newly annexed underdeveloped areas by means of an incremental taxing system.[20]

The Governor's Commission

The Governor's Commission on Metropolitan Area Problems was a top-level group of 20 business, labor, and professional leaders with particular expertise in urban problems. As a basis for discussion at commission meetings, a critical paper, *Local Governmental Boundaries and Areas: New Policies for California* was prepared by Stanley Scott, University of California, Berkeley,

Lewis Keller, League of California Cities staff, and
John C. Bollens, University of California, Los Angeles.
The paper was subsequently republished in a variety of
forms.[21]

It proposed a state-level commission of five members appointed by the governor, to review all annexation, incorporation, and special district formation
proposals. The commission could be located in the
governor's office, or in the State Department of Finance, or it could be independent. The commission's
actions could be governed by standards specified in
the statute, some mandatory and some discretionary. The
position paper also listed factors that the commission
should consider in arriving at decisions; they were
incorporated verbatim in the LAFCo legislation, and appear in paragraph 54796 of the *California Government
Code*.

While the major power proposed for the commission
was that of review, it is a tribute to the vision of
the authors that they recognized the necessity for
the commission to engage in planning and initiating
proposals as well. Further, the report considered
realistically problems of initiation of jurisdiction,
factual investigation by the agency staff, notice, formal hearings, agency action, judicial review, and enforcement. The procedures of a number of other states
and countries were included in an appendix.

Attorney General's Views

The suggestion of the state attorney general was
similar to that of the Governor's Commission. The
office of the attorney general handles quo warranto
actions, the final legal effort to block annexations
and incorporations that have already been completed. As
the agency in contact with all of the most questionable
proposals, the attorney general's office was acutely
aware of the problems arising from the existing system.
The office suggested the creation of viable statewide

or regional agencies to review annexation and incorporation proposals. Such agencies would cure what the
attorney general considered to be the "paramount evil"
of the existing system: the fact that city councils
"sit as judge, fact finder, and administrator in...
[annexation] proceedings."[22]

Two Proposals and a Compromise

The form in which the LAFCo legislation was finally
introduced reflected the deep divisions in political
philosophy and approach among the groups concerned.[23]
The legislation was offered as two separate bills. Assembly Bill 1662, introduced by Assemblyman Knox, reflected the views of the Governor's Commission on
Metropolitan Area Problems and the testimony of other
proponents of a strong, state level commission. It proposed a state level commission to control formations.

Senate Bill 861 was introduced by state Senator
Eugene Nisbet, who took an active role in shaping policy,
and reflected to some extent the views of CSAC and other
home-rule forces. The senate bill proposed county-
level commissions to review annexation. The commissions
were to be composed of two county and two city members
and one public member. Initially it was hoped that if
the assembly bill passed, the functions suggested in
the senate bill could be assigned to the same state-
level commission.

After the first hearing on the assembly bill, pressures from CSAC forced a compromise. Finally CSAC, the
league, the governor's office, and the assembly committee agreed that both formations and annexations should
be reviewed by the sort of county level board suggested
in the senate annexation bill. With both CSAC and league backing, the measures passed despite continuing attempts to emasculate them by giving LAFCos advisory
powers only, or by making legislation permissive rather
than mandatory.

THE LAFCO LEGISLATION

The statute that finally emerged from the process of hearings, special reports, debate, and compromise is a unique synthesis of regulatory powers. Before describing the provisions of the statute, it is important to examine the elements that distinguish it from all other state regulatory schemes.

Five features merit commentary: (1) LAFCos are located at the county level. (2) They draw together city and county politicians as well as representatives of the public. This "political" body also receives expert "technical" assistance. (3) LAFCos integrate review of all the most important types of local governmental structure change: city annexations (both uninhabited and inhabited), city incorporations, city disincorporations, and various changes in special districts including formations, dissolutions, annexations of additional territory to existing districts, detachments, consolidations, and reorganizations. (LAFCos have no jurisdiction over school districts and until 1967 had no jurisdiction over county service areas. There are also minor limitations on their jurisdiction over certain other types of districts.) (4) They are empowered and encouraged to make studies and plans as well as merely to review problems that come to them on an ad hoc basis. (5) Their decisions are subject to no significant review by higher bodies or courts.

This collection of attributes means that they are powerful instruments of "regional home rule": more local than state government, but better equipped to deal with areawide problems than city or county government alone.

Locating the Commission's Power

While the location of LAFCos at the county level was a political compromise and something of a retreat from the original idea of a state-level commission, it

can be argued strongly that the county is the correct
level for the function. Because many of the problems
that come before LAFCos concern very small changes in
existing conditions, a detailed knowledge of the local
area is essential. Placing the review function at the
state level would make more difficult the weighing of
local political and technical conditions. On the other
hand, locating it in an area geographically smaller
than the county would tend to make the commissions
overly parochial and unable to give adequate consideration to areawide interests.

Assigning the review function to the county level,
at least initially, was a wise choice, subject to two
qualifications. First, county lines in California were
drawn early in the state's history and often bear no
reasonable relationship to subsequent patterns of urbanization. While it is safe to say that the level of review is appropriate, this does not mean that LAFCos
operate within optimal jurisdictional lines. Second,
while the level of review is appropriate for the vast
bulk of cases, in the relatively rare situations where
there are incorporation proposals, a complex set of
district reorganizations, or overlapping and conflicting
annexation proposals submitted in the same area, sophis-
ticated economic and technical analysis is required for
good decisions. In such cases, most LAFCo staffs do
not have the time and expertise for elaborate analyses.
Therefore, a state-level review board for the appeal of
the most complex cases would be an improvement. (See
Ch. V, section on A State-Level Review Board.)

The fact that LAFCos include politicians from both
cities and counties, as well as public members, guarantees that the commissions will be sensitive to the political realities of the areas in which they are working. LAFCos, in addition, have executive officers who
can develop expertise by processing a large volume of
proposals. Further, the commissions may rely upon
"technical" support from cther county departments, or
occasionally from private consultants. This support

guarantees a certain amount of detached analysis to supplement the more visceral political judgments.

The fact that LAFCos combine review functions over all the most important types of local governments' structural change is of critical significance. For the first time it is possible for a single review entity to weigh alternative methods of providing local services, and to work out comprehensive strategies for the governmental structure of an entire area.

The legislation's strong emphasis upon making studies and cooperating with other planning bodies has provided an impetus for a new type of planning. (See Ch. IV, The Future of Urban Planning.) Thus the commissions can guide the thrust of development rather than merely disposing of cases on an ad hoc basis.

Finally all of these important powers are given real significance by the fact that LAFCos make final decisions. There is no system of appeals, special exceptions, "variances" or the like. Unless there is an unusual situation, courts will not review LAFCo decisions; or if such review is available, it will be extremely limited in scope. Perhaps at some point in the future a plantiff may successfully argue that a LAFCo decision was corruptly influenced, or that it was made with such defective evidence that it cannot stand, but so far this has not happened.

The Knox-Nisbet Act

The Knox-Nisbet Act, the statute setting out LAFCos' powers and duties, became operative on September 20, 1963. LAFCos were functioning in all counties (except, as noted, the City and County of San Francisco) by April 1, 1964.[24]

The daily work is carried out by the LAFCo executive officer, who is usually a county employee with one or more other jobs.[25] The executive officer relies upon county staff for technical assistance.

The commission consists of five members who convene periodically to make decisions on the basis of applications, executive officers' reports, and oral testimony presented at their hearings.[26] A section of the Knox-Nisbet Act provides for the creation and composition of the commission as follows:

> There is hereby created in each county a local agency formation commission. Except as provided in sections 54781 and 54782 the commission shall consist of five members, selected as follows:[27]
>
> (a) Two representing the county, appointed by the board of supervisors from their own membership. The board of supervisors shall appoint a third supervisor who shall be an alternate member of the commission. He is authorized to serve in place of any supervisor on the commission who is absent or who disqualifies himself from participating in a meeting of the commission.
>
> (b) Two representing the cities of the county, each of whom shall be a city officer, appointed by the city selection committee.[28]
>
> (c) One representing the general public, appointed by the other four members of the commission.[29]

In 1968 a bill was introduced in the California
Legislature proposing to expand the commission by adding
two representatives of special districts.[30] The bill
did not pass. Such a modification of the commission's
composition would have created many problems and greatly
weakened the LAFCos' effectiveness. For example, presumably many district board members on LAFCos would prefer to provide services by creating new special districts
or expanding existing districts. As already indicated,
further proliferation of special district governments is
undesirable. (See section on Controlling the Proliferation of Special Districts, in Ch. III.)

In addition, there are other objections to the presence of special district representatives. For example,
while both city and county governments are multifunctional political bodies, many special districts are not.
Their board members frequently lack the overview and
multifunctional approach needed in dealing with problems
assigned to LAFCos. Further, it has been demonstrated
that directors of special districts do not have the same
type of popular electoral support as that enjoyed by
elected officials of cities and counties. Consequently,
district board members do not have the same exposure to
competing community pressures.

Finally, the problem of devising a rational system
for selecting representatives of special districts within a county is very great. Clearly, tiny districts ser-
ving single developers should not be given voices equal
to those of very large districts (such as sanitation districts), but the problems of establishing equity in the
representation of districts are almost impossible to
solve, given existing variations in size and functions.

LAFCos are specifically given the power:

To review and approve or disapprove, with
or without amendment, wholly, partially, or
conditionally proposals for:

(1) The incorporation of cities;

(2) The formation of special districts; and

(3) The annexation of territory to local agencies...provided that the commission shall not impose any conditions which would regulate land use or subdivision requirements;

(4) The exclusion of territory from a city;

(5) The disincorporation of a city.[31]

They are also explicitly given the power to make studies, and are encouraged to ask for land use information, studies, and plans of cities, counties, and special districts.[32] In addition, LAFCos can adopt standards and procedures to be used in evaluating proposals on which they are to rule.[33] These provisions are the heart of LAFCos' powers.

The District Reorganization Act of 1965

The powers of LAFCos were enhanced by the passage of the District Reorganization Act of 1965, an elaborate piece of legislation setting forth a unified procedure for rationalizing the pattern of special district governments in California.[34] The act is designed to deal comprehensively with laws relating to the mass of existing special districts, and is highly complex. In essence, it (1) makes it easier to initiate proposals for eliminating or radically modifying districts that are anachronistic; (2) provides a mechanism (reorganization committees) that can effectively study and recommend needed changes; and (3) gives LAFCos the power to hold hearings and make final disposition of various kinds of organizational changes.

Some of the act's major provisions can be outlined as follows. Preliminary proceedings may be initiated in two ways: (1) by petition signed by district residents; or (2) by "resolution of application" made by the legislative body of any affected county, city, or district.

Under method (1), initiation by petition, the number of signatures required depends upon three factors. The first factor is the type of district. "Resident voter" district acts provide that registered voters residing within the district are entitled to vote in district matters. On the other hand, "landowner voter" district acts provide that only owners of land within the district are entitled to vote in the elections for district officers. The second factor is the type of change sought. Change may relate to (a) organization, including annexation, detachment, minor boundary change, consolidation, dissolution for inactivity, or merger; or, it may deal with (b) reorganization including one or more changes of organization proposed for each of two or more subject districts or any combination, with all such changes of organization and formation pursuant to a single plan of reorganization.

The third factor depends on whether the initiation is mandatory or permissive. When a mandatory initiation is filed and certified, a duty is imposed upon the commission to hold a hearing and make determinations concerning the proposal. A permissive initiation allows the commission to exercise discretionary power to deny the proposal without notice or hearing.

Method of initiation (2), "resolution of application" by a legislative body, differs from initiation by petition only as the terms imply. Under the second method, the legislative body acts; under the first, the voters act by affixing their signatures to petitions.

Once a permissive (nonmandatory) change of organization or reorganization is initiated, a reorganization committee of special district representatives is constituted. The committee studies the situation, prepares a report and makes recommendations. The Local Agency Formation Commission receives the petitions or applications, supervises the operations of the reorganization committee, holds hearings on the proposal, and makes the final disposition of the case.

In sum, the attributes and powers described in this chapter distinguish LAFCos from all other existing regulatory entities. The remaining chapters analyze the effects of the LAFCos' operations.

NOTES

CHAPTER I

1. Donald Foley, Ronald L. Drake, David W. Lyon and Bernardo A. Ynzenga, *Characteristics of Metropolitan Growth in California* (Berkeley: University of California, Institute of Urban and Regional Development: Center for Planning and Development Research, December 1965), p. 8.

2. *California Government Code* §34304. The requirement for 500 voters was inserted in 1959 to apply only to Los Angeles County. At that time San Diego, the next largest county, had a population of 1,033,011.

3. John C. Bollens, "Metropolitan and Fringe Area Developments," Tables of Annexations of One-Fourth Square Mile or More; annually 1954-1964 in *Municipal Year Book* (Chicago: International City Managers Association).

4. Robert O. Warren, *Government in Metropolitan Regions: A Reappraisal of Fractionated Political Organization* (Davis: University of California, Institute of Governmental Affairs, 1966), pp. 191-192.

5. Ibid., p. 201.

6. John Goldbach, "Boundary Change in California: The Local Agency Formation Commissions." Ms. to be published by Institute of Governmental Affairs, University of California at Davis. Chapter 1, p. 5.

7. State of California, Assembly, Interim Committee Reports 1959-1961 (Volume 6, Number 15) Final Report of the Assembly Interim Committee on Municipal and County Government, *Special District Problems in the State of California*, p. 11.

8. Ibid., p. 7.

9. Consider for example:

(a) *Sierra Lakes County Water District*: 2,600 acres near Soda Springs in Placer County. Formed in 1961 by petition of the developer, his wife, and four employees. The land was originally purchased for $5,000 cash and $195,000 in notes. The district proceeded to issue $800,000 in general obligation bonds and $700,000 in special assessment bonds.

(b) *Hidden Valley Water District*: in Ventura County. Formed by owners of weekend houses for the express purpose of providing *no* water to nearby land which was ripe for subdivision. (c)

(c) *Embarcadero Municipal Improvement District*: in Santa Barbara County. The developers who dominated this district were involved in various complex "padding" and "kickback" arrangements. They were convicted in a lower court of 30 counts of violations of the corporations code and grand theft. On appeal many of these convictions were reversed, but that situation is illustrative of the type of criminal or quasi-criminal activities which may occur.

10. John C. Bollens, *Special District Governments in the United States* (Berkeley: University of California Press, 1957), p. 114.

11. *Adjusting Municipal Boundaries: Law and Practice* (Washington, D.C.: Department of Urban Studies, National League of Cities, December 1966), pp. 291-301. See esp. p. 298. Cited hereafter as *Adjusting Municipal Boundaries*.(Note: This is a revised edition of the report published by Robert G. Dixon and John R. Kerstetter in 1959, *Adjusting Municipal Boundaries: The Law and Practice in 48 States*.) The study includes an exhaustive review of all state practices.

12. Ibid., pp. 291-292.

13. Ibid., pp. 298-299.

14. Ibid. See pp. 83-85.

15. Ibid., pp. 308-323.

16. State of California, Assembly, Interim Committee Reports, 1953-1955. Volume 6, Number 3. Final Report of the Assembly Interim Committee on Municipal and County Government, *Annexation and Related Problems*.

17. Ibid., pp. 7, 10-11.

18. State of California, Assembly, Interim Committee Reports 1955-1957 (Volume 6, Number 4) *Special Districts*; also Reports 1957-1959 (Volume 6 Number 12) *Special Districts in the State of California: Problems in General and the Consolidation of Sewer and Fire District Acts*; and Reports 1959-1961 (Volume 6, Number 15) *Special District Problems in the State of California*.

19. State of California, Assembly, Interim Committee Reports 1959-1961 (Volume 6, Number 16) Final Report of the Assembly Interim Committee on Municipal and County Government, *Annexation and Related Incorporation Problems in the State of California*. This is the single most important document on LAFCo history. It summarizes the findings of two hearings (in San Diego in January 1960, and in Oakland in May 1960) and contains the prepared statements of the League of California Cities and the County Supervisors Association of California.

20. James L. Clark and Louis F. Weschler, *Cross-County Annexation by Municipal Corporations in California* (Davis: University of California, Institute of Governmental Affairs, August 1965). California Government Series No. 8.

21. Extracts are printed in the report cited in note 19 above, *Annexation and Related Incorporation Problems*... as representing the position of the Governor's Commission. A condensed version was reprinted in the Commission's 1961 publication, *Metropolitan California*. In February 1961 it was reprinted in full by the Bureau of Public Administration at Berkeley in the Legislative Problems series.

22. *Annexation and Related Incorporation Problems*... (note 19 above), pp. 52-60. See esp. p. 54.

23. For a concise report on the politics of the two bills see William E. Glennon, "New Control Over Municipal Formation and Annexation," IV *Santa Clara Lawyer* 123-135 (1963-64).

24. *California Government Code* §54773-54799.

25. Intergovernmental Council on Urban Growth, *Report on a Statewide Survey of Local Agency Formation Commissions 1966* (Sacramento: 1966). This report is also referred to as *LAFCo 1966* and as the I.C.U.G. Study.

Pages 36-37 contain a list showing the LAFCo's executive officer in each county.

A more recent survey conducted by Fred Christiansen of the Sacramento LAFCo found that in 20 of the most active LAFCos, time is devoted to LAFCo executive work as follows:

(1) Administrative Analyst IV 80 percent
(2) Associate Planner 30 percent
(3) Principle Administrative Analyst 67 percent
(4) Director of Intergovernmental Services
    30 percent
(5) Associate Administrative Analyst 50 percent
(6) LAFCo Executive Officer 100 percent
(7) Principle Administrative Analyst 33 percent
(8) Senior Administrative Analyst 100 percent
(9) County Administrative Officer 1 percent /
    Senior Administrative Analyst 20 percent

(10) County Administrator 0 percent / Assistant
County Administrator 15 percent
(11) Chief Administrative Officer 3 percent /
Assistant Administrative Officer 33 percent
(12) County Executive 0 percent / Executive
Assistant 15 percent
(13) County Executive 0 percent / Information
Officer 70 percent
(14) County Administrator 3 percent / Administrative Analyst III 30 percent
(15) County Administrative Officer 10 percent /
Administrative Analyst 10 percent
(16) County Administrative Officer 10 percent /
Senior Administrative Analyst 60 percent
(17) Senior Planner 13 percent / Stenographer
III 100 percent
(18) County Clerk 25 percent / Clerk of the Board
25 percent
(19) Clerk of the Board 10 percent / Deputy
Executive Officer 100 percent
(20) County Administrative Officer 3 percent /
Assistant Administrative Officer 33 percent

26. See State of California, Assembly, Interim
Committee Reports 1964-1965 (Volume 6, Number 22: 3)
Operations of the Local Agency Formation Commissions.
Appendix tabulates the frequency with which the LAFCos
in the different counties meet.

27. See also *California Government Code* §54781
which provides in *Composition In County Without A City*:
If there is no city in the county, the commission shall
consist of five members, selected as follows:

(a) Three representing the county, appointed by
the board of supervisors from their own
membership. The board of supervisors shall
appoint a fourth supervisor who shall be an
alternate member of the commission. He is
authorized to serve in place of any supervisor on the commission who is absent or

who disqualifies himself from participating
in a meeting of the commission.

(b) Two representing the general public, appointed by the other three members of the
commission.

See also *California Government Code* §54782 which
provides in *Composition In County With One City*: If
there is only one city in the county, the commission
shall consist of five members, selected as follows:

(a) Two representing the county, appointed by
the board of supervisors from their own membership. The board of supervisors shall appoint a third supervisor who shall be an
alternate member of the commission. He is
authorized to serve in place of any supervisor on the commission who is absent or who
disqualifies himself from participating in
a meeting of the commission.

(b) One representing the city, who shall be a
city officer, appointed by the legislative
body of the city.

(c) Two representing the general public, appointed by the other three members of the
commission.

28. See also *California Government Code* §54784 which
provides in *City Selection Committee; meetings; appoint-
ments; alternate members:*

In each county containing two or more cities,
there shall be a city selection committee consisting of the mayor of each city within such
county, or, where there is no mayor, the chairman or president of the city legislative body.
A majority of the members of each city selection committee shall constitute a quorum.

The city selection committee shall meet at the
call of the local agency formation commission

chairman, or at the request of 60 percent of
the members of the city selection committee to
fill vacancies in the commission.

The city selection committee shall appoint one
alternate member to the commission in the same
manner as it appoints a regular member. If one
of the regular city members is absent from a
commission meeting, or disqualifies himself from
participating in a meeting, or is automatically
disqualified from participating therein pursuant
to this section, the alternate member is authorized to serve in his place for the meeting.
When the commission is considering a proposal
for the annexation of territory to a city of
which one of the members of the commission is
an officer, the member is disqualified from
participating in the proceedings of the commission with respect to the proposal and the
alternate member shall serve in his place for
such purpose.

29. From *California Government Code* §54780.

30. Senate Bill No. 783. Introduced by Senator
Miller, April 3, 1968. The critical additions to the
LAFCo statute would read:

§54780.(c) In counties containing two or more
special districts which have elected
boards, two representing such special
districts, each of whom shall be a special district board member, appointed by
the special district selection committee.

§54784.2   In each county containing two or more
special districts with elected boards
there shall be a special district selection committee consisting of the chairman of each such special district board.

31. *California Government Code* §54790.

32. *California Government Code* §54774.

33. *California Government Code* §54790(4)(b).

34. *California Government Code* §56000-58908.

CHAPTER II

A Quantitative Performance Profile of
Local Agency Formation Commissions

The preceding chapter has explained what Local
Agency Formation Commissions are and how they came to
be established. Chapters III and IV explain in greater
detail what they do. This chapter deals with three
basic questions: (1) What is the workload of the LAFCos?
How many proposals are there of what types, and how complex are they? (2) How have LAFCos disposed of them?
What percentage of each type of proposal is accepted,
rejected, or termed conditional? (3) What has been the
impact of LAFCos in quantitative terms? The inquiry
involves a comparison of past and current patterns of
annexation, incorporation, and special district formation.

A WORD OF CAUTION

Many qualitative complexities lurk in any quantitative table of LAFCo actions. Some annexations, some
incorporations, and some special district formations
are good and some are bad, but aggregate tables do not
discriminate between them. One important function of
LAFCos is to deter questionable actions, If LAFCos are

truly effective, many of the worst proposals will not be submitted. In addition, many applications are screened out as unacceptable and informally disapproved by the LAFCo staff prior to formal submission. This review function, of course, does not appear in formal tables of LAFCo activity. This chapter must therefore be read in conjunction with the next two, while care must be taken to avoid ascribing too much significance to mere numbers.

SOME OVERALL FIGURES

An examination of the total number of proposals studied by all LAFCos throughout the state shows that the overwhelming majority are of two types: (1) proposals for annexations of uninhabited lands to cities, and (2) proposals for annexations of additional territory to existing special districts. Together these have accounted for an estimated 94 percent of all those submitted.[1]

All other possible types of LAFCo action (incorporation, inhabited city annexations, special district formation, special district detachment, special district dissolution, special district reorganization, city detachment, and city disincorporation) together account for the other six percent. While these are aggregate state figures, they represent a pattern that is fairly constant in each county.

Annexations: Inhabited or Uninhabited?

Inhabited annexations to cities are much less common than the uninhabited in California, for three basic reasons. (1) California requires that (a) there be an election for an inhabited annexation, and (b) that the majority of residents in the area to be annexed approve the action. Procedure is cumbersome, slow, and expensive.

(2) Annexation may increase the taxes of residents
of annexed areas, because cities typically provide more
services than unincorporated areas do. Such tax increases do not, however, necessarily occur in all cases.
Economies of scale may make it cheaper for an area to
annex to a city that provides a variety of efficiently
managed services than to remain unincorporated and depend on costly services from a number of inefficient
districts. (3) A circumstance regarded unfavorably by
persons in annexed territory is the fact that annexation usually will require the annexed minority to abide
by decisions made by the city majority. Thus, because
of these and other hazards and uncertainties, only 12
percent of all city annexation proposals involved inhabited territory.[2]

Districts

Special district formations, dissolutions, reorganizations, consolidations, and detachments are frequently related. A new multifunctional district may be
created to take the place of two single function districts; or, one district may be dissolved only to be
reconstituted immediately as a slightly different type
of district. Aggregate state figures indicate that the
number of special districts in California continues to
rise at the rate of about 100 per year. (See Table
VIII.) However, aggregate data hide distinctions in
the categories of districts formed (e.g., independent
v. dependent). Also, recent data indicate that the
District Reorganization Act of 1965 will be effective
in rationalizing special district structure in California and somewhat reducing the number of total districts. (See Table XII.)

New Cities

Since LAFCos were created, only eight new California cities (which have been subjected to LAFCo

review), have been incorporated in California.[3] City detachments are quite rare, with only five city detachments in the state during 1966. There has been only one city disincorporation since LAFCos came into effect.

The total number of actions does not, of course, indicate the relative importance of the various proposals, nor does it give an accurate picture of the way in which LAFCos spend their time. A good deal of LAFCo time is spent on useful background studies which do not involve any specific proposal.

General Observations

Proposals demanding the least expenditure of time and energy for investigation include annexation of uninhabited areas to cities, as well as annexations of additional territory to special districts. Most of the latter involve only very small areas. A typical example would be a petition to extend the boundary of a water district to include a dozen new houses in a subdivision, where water is needed and no alternate source is available.

Inhabited city annexations almost always require more time, more intensive analysis, and finer political sensitivities. The few proposals that relate to incorporations and complex district reorganizations are usually both time-consuming and strenuous. Finally, both painstaking analysis and political sensitivity are required when conflicting proposals are offered for the same land. A good example is the case of the Dominguez-Carson area in Los Angeles County, where at one time four annexation proposals overlapped an incorporation proposal and/or each other.[4]

CITY ANNEXATIONS

Because the bulk of California's population increase is occurring on the fringes of existing cities, much of the LAFCos' workload consists of proposals for the annexation of such fringe land to cities. The commissions usually regard annexation proposals favorably.

Types of Territory

To understand the extent of this activity, it is helpful to know how many city annexation proposals there have been; what proportion of all proposals are of this type; and how many involved inhabited territory, and how many uninhabited territory. As noted earlier, the LAFCo study conducted by the Intergovernmental Council on Urban Growth indicated that by the summer of 1966, 2,540 or 47 percent of the 5,414 proposals examined, were city annexation proposals. Close to 90 percent of these applied to the annexation of uninhabited land.

The "inhabited-uninhabited" dichotomy is a bit deceptive. Frequently, uninhabited annexations concern land that is ripe for subdivision and is immediately subdivided and developed after annexation. While few in number, the inhabited annexations may be large in size. For example, between 1955 and 1967, the average number of people per city annexation was over 1,000. (If the data in Table III are reliable, the total population involved in the annexations was 592,892, and the total number of city annexations was 560. Thus the average annexation per city included about 1,059 people.) Finally, by gerrymandering boundaries so that the area includes fewer than 12 registered voters and thus is legally "uninhabited," and by taking territory incrementally by "piecemeal" annexation, proponents are able to avoid the statutory requirements of an election and can annex substantial populated fringe land with minimum formality.

The great variety in the physical size of parcels taken by annexation is illustrated by Table I, drawn from data collected on all LAFCo operations through September 30, 1964. Note that total uninhabited

TABLE I

Number and Size of City Annexation Proposals in Seven Urban California Counties Considered by LAFCos Through September 30, 1964[5]

County	Uninhabited			Inhabited		
	No.	Acreage	Average	No.	Acreage	Average
Alameda	15	1,749	116	2	116	58
Contra Costa	48	7,064	148	6	763	127
Los Angeles	98	8,325	65	19	2,649	39
San Bernardino	52	8,969	65	-	-	-
San Diego	39	5,518	142	16	30,719	1,924
Santa Clara	70	6,508	39	-	-	-
Ventura	60	2,000	33	1	7	7

acreage ranges from 1,749 in Alameda County to 8,969 in San Bernardino County, and "inhabited" acreage from 7 in Ventura County to 30,719 in San Diego County.

Results of Decisions

Another major question relates to the way LAFCos have disposed of proposals: What percentage has been approved, conditionally approved, or disapproved? As a general rule, LAFCos favor the extension of municipal services by municipalities wherever feasible. Unless a proposed annexation is clearly premature, oddly shaped, or designed to take land that is valuable for taxes only and that would leave undesirable parcels, it will usually be approved by a LAFCo.

TABLE II

LAFCo Disposition of City Annexation Proposals
1963-1966[6]

Year	Approved	Conditionally Approved	Disapproved
1963-1964	865	122	16
1965	839	104	33
1966	509	38	14

Roughly 98 percent of all proposals were approved. While this tally demonstrates that LAFCos were favorable to annexations, it does not imply an abdication of regulatory power. As indicated earlier, many of the most questionable types of annexations are no longer attempted now that LAFCos exist, because they are sure to fail; therefore they do not show up in statistics. In addition, the "disapproved" figure does not include proposals submitted but later withdrawn, or proposals that were informally disapproved by LAFCo staff members in advance of actual submission. In practice, permitting a withdrawal is a polite way of allowing a proponent to avoid flat disapproval. Figures from San Bernardino County (whose profile of city annexations roughly parallels the state profile) indicate that inclusion of withdrawal figures would double the number of annexations that were actually disapproved.[7] Of greatest significance is the fact that roughly 10 percent of all city annexations are now approved conditionally. This record shows substantial policing by LAFCos. In most cases, the conditions of approval have forced the proponents to enlarge, contract, or shift the borders of the proposed annexation to improve the shape so that it is easier to service. Often, the changes also provide more equitable distributions of property and sales tax burdens and benefits (as noted in Ch. III).

Assessing the Impact of LAFCos

Turning next to an assessment of the impact LAFCos have had upon city annexations in California, it is necessary to examine the pattern of city annexations before the advent of LAFCos, and to compare them with the subsequent record. (See Table III.)

The figures in Table III indicate that there is no simple correlation between the creation of LAFCos and changes in the aggregate number of cities annexing territory in any given year, the total number of annexations, the total number of square miles of territory annexed per year, or the total population annexed per year. Such findings do not mean, however, that LAFCos have failed to rationalize such factors as the tempo, sequence, and pattern of development, as well as others that do not show in the aggregate figures. Subsequent chapters, particularly the section concerned with spheres of influence, indicate that LAFCos have been effective.

TABLE III

Number and Characteristics of City Annexations in California
1955-1967

Year	# Cities Annexing	# Annexations	Square Miles	Population
1955	38	477	59.92	64,476
1956	40	387	30.85	31,347
1957	35	327	91.82	42,139
1958	29	259	100.03	35,281
1959	42	579	102.77	43,862
1960	44	589	100.40	54,576
1961	46	491	81.33	107,996
1962	48	549	107.44	34,066
1963	48	486	63.35	26,431
1964	44	319	71.35	46,548
1965	56	398	52.24	32,815
1966	50	417	83.04	52,885
1967	40	446	73.37	20,470
[Totals]	560			592,892]

INCORPORATIONS

As indicated earlier, another major purpose of LAFCos is to review incorporation proposals so as to prevent those that are ill-advised from proceeding further. Is there a difference between the patterns of incorporation before and after the establishment of LAFCos?

The LAFCo law went into effect on September 20, 1963. Since that date, 17 California cities have been incorporated, of which eight were subject to LAFCo review.[9] The other nine incorporations were initiated before the LAFCo law became effective, and therefore were not reviewed by the commissions.

In the case of a city incorporation, it makes little sense to speak of LAFCo "acceptance" or "rejection" of an incorporation proposal, because the review process involves long negotiation both before and after the proposal is submitted.

The central problem is to determine what, if any, effect LAFCos have had on the quality of city incorporations. As noted in the discussion in Chapter I, many incorporation proposals prior to the LAFCos were "defensive," and created weak cities. Many others related to "special interest" cities. Has LAFCo changed this pattern? The answer may lie in an analysis of select characteristics of cities incorporated before and after LAFCos.

Some Assumptions

The premises underlying the following tables are as follows: A small population is likely to indicate a weak new governmental entity. In urban areas, an incorporation with a small population is usually defensive, i.e., designed to prevent annexation of the territory by a contiguous city. It is likely to breed inefficiency, inequality in taxes and services, and lack of coordination.

TABLE IV

Select Characteristics of Sample Cities Chosen from All Those Incorporated Prior to the LAFCos

City	Year	County	Population When Incorporated	Assessed Valuation	Per Capita Assessed Valuation
Cabazon	1955	Riverside	855	$ 650,290	$ 760
Anderson	1956	Shasta	4,246	3,407,760	811
Bradbury	1957	Los Angeles	810	1,996,760	2,465
Irwindale	1957	Los Angeles	700	9,962,870	14,232
Rolling Hills Estates	1957	Los Angeles	4,000	5,429,150	1,357
Grover City	1959	San Luis Obispo	2,750	4,741,010	1,724
Cudahy	1960	Los Angeles	2,500	8,455,265	3,382
Bell Gardens	1961	Los Angeles	26,000	18,833,430	724
Weed	1961	Siskiyou	3,500	2,243,045	640
San Marcos	1963	San Diego	3,200	7,014,910	2,192

In rural areas--particularly if the city is isolated, incorporation of an area with a small population is not likely to generate as many problems. Similarly a reasonably large assessed valuation is a good indication that a community will be able to provide itself with adequate and desired public services. Assessed valuation, particularly per capita assessed valuation, is also a good indicator of the equitability of government financing. Note, for example, the grossly distorted per capita assessed valuation figures of the classic "tax shelter" cities such as Industry and Commerce in Table V.

Table IV summarizes some critical characteristics of a systematic sample of cities incorporated during the eight years before LAFCos.[10]

Tax Shelters and Special Interest Incorporations

Among the cities incorporated prior to the LAFCos, a number could be described as tax shelter cities. This specialized group has a set of characteristics strikingly different from those shown in Table IV.

The list in Table V by no means exhausts the special interest incorporations in California. For example, the City of Vernon, which was incorporated in 1905, by the fiscal year 1963-1964 had a population of 229 and an assessed valuation of $257,863,040.[11] Thus the residents enjoyed an assessed valuation of more than a million dollars per capita.

The inequities involved in such tax shelter cities are apparent. It has been persuasively argued that entities that are nominally cities, but that have very few residents, are shelters that pervert the concept of responsible and responsive city government. The resulting high per capita assessed valuations permit low tax rates. Further, "industrial" cities receive sizable state sales tax subventions. These factors

TABLE V

Select Characteristics of Certain Special Interest (Tax Shelter) Cities Incorporated in California Prior to the LAFCos[12]

City	Year	County	Population When Incorporated	Assessed Valuation	Per Capita Assessed Valuation
Dairyland	1955	Orange	550	$ 1,746,770	$ 3,175
Industry	1957	Los Angeles	625	18,888,680	30,223
Irwindale	1957	Los Angeles	700	9,962,870	14,232
Commerce	1960	Los Angeles	8,300	172,495,520	20,782

help create clusterings of industry in locations that are rational only in terms of tax advantages to affected businesses and industries, but are irrational if evaluated according to optimum land use, potential impact on unemployment, topography, relationship to transportation facilities, or other reasonable bases of determining urban service boundaries.

LAFCo Review

As we have seen, Table IV deals with characteristics of a sample of all cities incorporated in California prior to LAFCos, and Table V with certain special interest cities from the same period. Table VI relates to cities incorporated since the advent of LAFCos, and provides material for comparison with the earlier groups.

While the numbers are too small for statistical significance, it is notable that (1) the numbers of incorporations per year appear to be diminishing; (2) there has been only one special interest incorporation (that of Indian Wells);[13] and (3) there do not appear to have been any defensive incorporations.

SPECIAL DISTRICTS

One of the principal reasons for creating the LAFCos was to control the proliferation of independent special districts, and to guarantee that any new districts were not only necessary, but also were coordinated with other existing governments. In 1965, with the passage of the District Reorganization Act, California went further and entrusted the LAFCos with responsibility for eliminating anachronistic districts and reorganizing those that had become partially obsolete.

TABLE VI

Select Characteristics of California Cities Whose Incorporation Has Been Reviewed by LAFCos[14]

City	Year Incorporated	County	Population When Incorporated	Assessed Valuation	Per Capita Assessed Valuation
Yountville	1965	Napa	5,400	$ 657,170	$ 121
Rio Del	1965	Humboldt	3,570	2,598,700	745
South Lake Tahoe	1965	El Dorado	10,000	54,017,610	5,401
California City	1965	Kern	600	9,191,060	15,318
Carpinteria	1965	San Bernardino	6,650	10,615,840	1,608
Scotts Valley	1966	Santa Cruz	3,500	6,051,540	1,729
Indian Wells	1967	Riverside	870	14,000,000[a]	16,500[a]
Yorba Linda	1967	Orange	12,000	23,000,000[a]	1,916[a]

[a]1969 figure.

The following analysis attempts to determine the number of actions involving special districts, what type they were, how LAFCos have disposed of them, and to what extent LAFCos have made a difference in the proliferation of special districts.

Creation of Districts

Between the creation of LAFCos and the cutoff date of the Intergovernmental Council on Urban Growth study in the summer of 1966, LAFCos dealt with 2,860 proposals involving special districts.[15] They included 2,522 proposals for annexation of additional territory to existing districts; 193 for new formations; 120 for district detachments; 16 for dissolutions; and 9 for reorganizations.

The District Reorganization Act had become effective only in 1965. A better indication of the relative proportions of proposals, therefore, is a more recent study of LAFCo actions affecting special districts in the nine Bay Area Counties between the time when the D.R.A. became effective in October 1965 and December of 1967. During that period, of the 370 actions involving special districts, 238 were annexations; 85, detachments; 29, dissolutions; 10, consolidations; and 8, formations.[16]

LAFCos appear to be less receptive to proposals for the formation of new special districts than to any other kinds of proposals concerning local agencies.

The rejection rate is thus roughly 9 to 13 percent, in sharp contrast to rates of 1 to 2 percent for rejection of city annexation proposals. These figures probably do not accurately reflect the real rejection rate figure for the same reasons that applied to city annexations: (1) the most questionable proposals are no longer even offered; (2) "withdrawn" proposals (tantamount to rejection) are not tallied; those that were screened out before formal submission are also excluded. If the withdrawal rate is as high as the rejection rate, actual

TABLE VII

LAFCo   Disposition of Proposals for
Special District Formations 1963-1966[17]

Year	Approved	Conditionally Approved	Rejected
1963-1964	67	14	7
1965	53	8	9
1966	53	8	9

rejections of special district formation proposals may
be running as high as 20 to 30 percent. Limited data
from San Bernardino County lend some weight to this
speculation.[18] It is also important to note that of
those formations approved, 10 percent were approved with
conditions, and in some instances the conditions are se-
vere. (See "Latent Powers" discussion in Ch. V.)

Total Numbers

Have LAFCos made a difference in the proliferation
of special districts? The following table shows changes
in the total numbers of special districts in California
before and after LAFCos. These figures represent a number of separate occurrences: new formations, dissolutions, and consolidations.

In general, Table VIII indicates that so far LAFCos
have not had a significant impact on total special district formations, although the D.R.A. may cause some
changes in the future.

In 1962-1963, just prior to passage of the Knox-
Nisbet Act, there was an apparent wave of special district formation caused by those interests in the state
who did not care to have their proposals reviewed. In
1963-1964 formations dropped drastically, but in 1964-
1965 the slack was taken up and the year saw the district total raised by 207.

TABLE VIII

Total Number of Special Districts in California
by Year, 1955-1967[19]

Year	Number	Change Number	Change Percent
1955-56	2,780	-	-
1956-57	2,887	+109	+3.9
1957-58	2,992	+ 93	+3.2
1958-59	3,038	+ 56	+1.9
1959-60	3,128	+ 56	+1.9
1960-61	3,178	+ 55	+1.8
1961-62	3,237	+ 59	+1.8
1962-63	3,342	+105	+3.2
1963-64	3,317	- 25	-0.8
1964-65	3,524	+207	+5.8
1965-66	3,628	+104	+2.9
1966-67	3,571	- 57	-0.6

Furthermore, an analysis of the growth patterns of
six types of special districts (as presented in Tables
IX and X) indicates that creation of LAFCos has not been
decisive in altering such patterns. An important dis-
tinction is that between "independent" special districts
(the classic special district) and "dependent" districts.
The latter type is controlled by county boards of supervisors or city councils and therefore does not create
the full range of problems presented by independent districts. Recent data on four Southern California counties
(collected by Herbert Hollandsworth, a student at San
Diego State College, in connection with a thesis) indicate that the aggregate growth in districts in the counties surveyed came largely from dependent districts, but
that the rate of new independent special district formations has declined.[20]

Aggregate figures do not show whether or not LAFCos
have affected the formation of districts with built-in
problems: inadequate size, overlapping jurisdictions,
and inability to provide services. A final judgment can
be made only after detailed analyses of districts formed
since the establishment of LAFCos. However, mere proliferation of districts per se (independent of whether
or not they were formed for a good purpose, are well managed, and directed by honest citizens), leads to situations in which it is virtually impossible to coordinate
development of an area. For this reason, it is disturbing that the numbers of special districts in California
have continued to grow.

Annexations to Existing Districts

About 47 percent of all proposals submitted to
LAFCos related to the annexation of territory to existing special districts. The great majority of these proposals were approved, as Table XI indicates:

TABLE IX

Cumulative Number of Select Types of Special Districts in California
1955-1967

	55-56	56-57	57-58	58-59	59-60	60-61	61-62	62-63	63-64	64-65	65-66	66-67
Fire Protection	450	458	463	451	455	458	460	469	470	469	465	463
Highway Lighting	411	416	421	429	426	423	400	392	404	385	383	371
Community Services	40	51	62	73	85	96	112	112	112	131	148	155
Public Utility	75	75	75	74	72	69	68	68	68	66	65	66
Recreation and Park	-	-	16	33	58	92	98	101	101	108	112	111
County Service Areas	12	16	25	29	35	45	75	110	110	211	291	332

TABLE X

Percentage Annual Growth of Select Types of Special Districts in California
1955-1967[1]

	55-56	56-57	57-58	58-59	59-60	60-61	61-62	62-63	63-64	64-65	65-66	66-67
Fire Protection	-	+1.7	+1.0	-2.6	+.9	+.7	+.4	+1.9	+.1	-.1	-.9	-.2
Highway Lighting	-	+1.2	+1.2	+1.9	-.7	-.7	-5.4	-1.9	+3.0	-4.7	-.5	-3.1
Community Services	-	+2.5	+11.6	+15	+16	+12.9	+16.4	-	-	+16.9	+12.9	+4.7
Public Utility	-	-	-	-1.4	-2.7	-4.1	-1.4	-	-	-3.0	-1.3	+1.3
Recreation and Park	-	-	-	+106.2	+75.7	+35.8	+6.5	+3.0	-	+6.8	+3.7	-.9
County Service Areas	-	+33.3	+56.3	+16	+20.7	+40	+66.6	+46.6	-	+90.9	+37.8	+14.0

56

TABLE XI

LaFCo Disposition of Proposals for the
Annexation of Additional Territory to
Existing Special Districts, 1963-1966[22]

Year	Approved	Conditionally Approved	Disapproved
1963-1964	1,189	118	10
1965	664	103	11
1966	358	63	6

As indicated earlier, the District Reorganization
Act of 1965 granted LAFCos additional powers to initiate
dissolutions, detachments, consolidations, and reorganizations of special districts. The Intergovernmental
Council on Urban Growth found that, under the D.R.A.,
LAFCos approved 89 detachments, 7 dissolutions, and 5
reorganizations in 1966. William Zion, the council's
consultant, has also completed an independent, unpublished
study of the impact of LAFCos on special districts in
the nine San Francisco Bay Area counties. His findings
for the period between October 1965 (when the D.R.A.
became effective) and December 1967 are summarized in
Table XII.

The eight districts created in the Bay Area included
two sanitary and two water districts, three community
service areas, and one county service area. The great
majority of annexations were concerned with water and
sanitary districts. Detachments, consolidations, reorganizations, and dissolutions took place for a number of
reasons, for example: (1) the districts had become
entirely nonfunctional; (2) new incorporations or city
annexations made it more reasonable for a city to provide
the service than for the district to do so; or (3) there
were overlaps of jurisdiction and duplication of functions.

TABLE XII

LAFCo Actions Under the District Reorganization Act in Bay Area Counties: October 1965-December 1967[23]

County	Formations	Annexations	Detachments	Consolidation/ Reorganization	Dissolutions
Alameda	-	32	2	1	5
Contra Costa	4	52	12	4	14
Marin	-	46	2	1	7
Napa	4	28	-	2	-
San Francisco	--------------------------------Not Under LAFCo Law--------------------------------				
San Mateo	-	23	4	1	1
Santa Clara	-	34	65	-	-
Solano	-	-	-	1	-
Sonoma	-	23	2	-	2
Totals	8	238	85	10	29

The actual number of detachments is somewhat higher than that shown, because a city (1) can detach territory from a fire district without LAFCo disapproval, and (2) automatically detaches territory from a county service area without LAFCo approval. Also LAFCos may require various district detachments as conditions for city annexations without listing them as separate proposals.

CONCLUSION

In this chapter we have examined a number of basic questions: What are the numbers and types of proposals LAFCos have dealt with? How have they disposed of them? What impact, if any, have LAFCo decisions had on the patterns of governmental structure change in California?

The aggregate figures on the proposals of each type subject to LAFCos' decisions are of interest in themselves, because they show the type of governmental reorganization going on in the state.

1. The fact that most changes now taking place in California are incremental annexations to existing special districts indicates that a state-level review board alone would be too remote from the local scene to be really effective.

2. The figures on the disposition of various types of proposals indicate the degree to which LAFCos deter certain types of plans, and give a fair indication of LAFCos' preferences. The clearest finding is that the commissions are inclined to approve proposals for annexations of territory to existing cities, and disinclined to approve the formation of additional special districts.

3. The figures comparing the pattern of annexation development before and after LAFCos are not revealing. The total number of cities that annex territory per year, the total number of annexations per year, the

total number of square miles of territory annexed per year, and the total population annexed per year did not change significantly as a result of LAFCos. There are not enough data to permit accurate evaluation of the impact LAFCos have had on incorporations, although the commissions apparently have approved neither special interest incorporations, nor purely defensive ones. The total number of special districts in the state has continued to grow in much the same manner despite LAFCos, although recent figures indicate that the District Reorganization Act will have a substantial impact in cutting down that number.

A troubling question remains: Do the essentially negative comparative findings indicate that LAFCos have not had an important effect? The answer is difficult to find. A dramatic drop in the number of district formations, or a statistically significant shift in the incorporation or annexation figures might provide a firmer base from which to argue the utility of LAFCos, but the lack of such a finding does not prove the reverse. The aggregate figures do not give an accurate picture of changes in the "healthiness" of given actions however that concept is defined. For example, they do not show whether a given proposal was timely, the right size, or related rationally to the social or economic fabric of area in which the change took place.

The next two chapters examine a number of things the progressive LAFCos have been doing. These findings are essentially positive.

NOTES

CHAPTER II

1. This estimate is based on the following information. First, the I.C.U.G. study covers the period from September 20, 1963, when LAFCos were established, to 1966. (The study's cutoff date varies between May and June 1966, but the variation is not critical because we are concerned here with the percentages of total proposals.) Forty LAFCos were operative by December 1, 1963; 52 by January 1, 1964; and all by April 1, 1964. LAFCos considered 5,414 proposals during the study period: 2,540 (47 percent) were city annexation proposals, both inhabited and uninhabited; 2,522 (47 percent) were annexations to existing special districts. Together, they totaled 94 percent.

Second, all proposals considered by LAFCos up to September 30, 1964 are noted in California, Assembly Interim Committee Reports 1963-1965 (Volume 6, Number 22: 3) *Operations of the Local Agency Formation Commissions*. The report indicates that 88 percent of all city annexations involved unincorporated territory. In general this study accepts the assumption that the patterns indicated in the two foregoing reports tend to remain constant.

2. This figure is based on material in the Assembly Report cited above, and includes data from September 20, 1963 to September 30, 1964.

3. See State of California, Office of the Controller, *Annual Report of Financial Transactions Concerning Cities of California, Fiscal Year 1966-67.*

4. The Dominguez-Carson area in Los Angeles County is an area of 32+ square miles, and contains a population of about 130,000.

In September 1966 the Los Angeles LAFCo denied an
incorporation proposal to form the new City of Dominguez
and ordered a staff study. On January 16, 1967 the
City of Compton filed a proposal to annex a large amount
of land in the area. On February 1, 1967 Long Beach
and Los Angeles simultaneously filed other annexation
proposals; in addition, a proposal was filed for
incorporating the separate City of Dominguez.

5. State of California, Assembly, Interim Committee Reports 1963-1965 (Volume 6, Number 22: 3)   Final Report of the Assembly Interim Committee on Municipal
and County Government, *Operations of the Local Agency
Formation Commissions*, pp. 65-69.

6. I.C.U.G. Study, p. 35.

7. San Bernardino County Local Agency Formation
Commission, *The First 500*, by Robert B. Rigney (January
1968), p. 33. Hereafter, *The First 500*.

8. Figures from 1955-1957 are from *Adjusting Municipal Boundaries* (Department of Urban Studies, National
League of Cities, 1959 edition only. See note 11,
Ch. I). The figures from 1958 to the present were com-
piled from the *Municipal Year Book*.

9. State of California, Office of the Controller,
*Annual Reports of Financial Transactions Concerning
Cities...; fiscal years 1963-64 to 1966-67.

10. To obtain the sample, all incorporations were
arranged alphabetically by year, and every fifth incorporation was selected.

Cities incorporated between January 1, 1955 and
September 20, 1963 (when the LAFCo law became effective)
are found in Appendix I.

11. See note 9 above; fiscal year 1962-63.

12. Ibid., fiscal years including 1955 through 1960.

13. Herbert Hollandsworth, a student at San Diego State College, conducted a study of the Indian Wells incorporation in the course of research for a thesis on LAFCos and concluded that the incorporation was both defensive and a special interest act.

14. Nine cities in California list dates of incorporation after the LAFCo law became effective (September 20, 1963), but were not reviewed by LAFCo because they were *initiated* earlier. (See list in Appendix II.)

15. I.C.U.G. Study, p. 35.

16. William Zion, unpublished study of the impact of LAFCos on special districts in the Bay Area. pp. 39-50.

17. I.C.U.G. Study, p. 35.

18. *The First 500*, p. 39. Of the special district formation proposals in San Bernardino County, 2 were approved, 2 were disapproved, and 3 were withdrawn. Thus, disapprovals and withdrawals outnumbered successful proposals by 5 to 2.

19. State of California, Office of the Controller, *Annual Report of Financial Transactions Concerning Special Districts...* Reports for fiscal years 1955-56 through 1966-67.

20. Letter, Herbert Hollandsworth to author.

21. Constructed from data in Table IX.

22. I.C.U.G. Study, p. 35.

23. See Zion, note 16 above, p. 50.

Policing Changes of Governmental Structure

As we have seen, in general the coming of the LAFCos has brought little change in the annual rate of annexations, incorporations, and special district formation. The significant feature of LAFCo activity appears to be their rejection of unacceptable proposals, and the imposing of conditions on others to eliminate undesirable provisions. But, more specifically, a number of questions remain: What types of annexations do LAFCos allow? How do they handle pressures brought by land developers? Can LAFCos serve as mediators in the most heated disputes? These questions and others will be examined in the next two chapters. The overall conclusion is that the more progressive LAFCos have made advances toward improving rationality in the extension of governmental services.

ELIMINATING RAIDS ON THE TAX BASE

In California as in other states, "tax base raiding" has been a major incentive for annexation. Such raiding expresses the desire of a municipality to annex land that will provide substantial tax revenues, but require a relatively low level of municipal service expenditure in return. It is not surprising that raids are often focused on industrial and commercial areas, because of their high assessments.

It is clear that industrial and commercial areas may be valuable to a community for at least two reasons. (1) The tax yield per acre on land supporting a department store or oil refinery is far higher than that on land developed for residential or marginal use. (2) The level of municipal expenditure on the first type of area is usually lower than on the second. The amounts of needed police and fire protection, of street lighting and water are frequently less. Further, business or industrial areas are not populated by large numbers of children who must be educated at the expense of the community.

The raided land is often oddly shaped, e.g., the strips, cherry stems, and pockets mentioned in Chapter I. A cherry stem typically drains off tax revenue that should be shared with the adjacent unincorporated area, the residence of many of those who patronize the shopping center at the middle of the "cherry." It is costly to provide service for pockets of unincorporated county land surrounded by a city or for strips of incorporated land that project from a city. But the disruptive effect is not limited to inefficiencies in services. Equally serious is the distortion of the pattern of growth of the area, so that new development locates in irrational places. Frequently these gerrymandered boundaries make it impossible adequately to finance new cities and thus block logical new incorporations.

Denials and Alterations

The better LAFCos have responded decisively to this problem. Many annexation proposals are disallowed because their dominant motive is a "tax raid." Most of the cases in which LAFCos propose an addition to or subtraction from territory proposed for annexation represent attempts to achieve more equitable distribution of tax burdens and benefits. For example, LAFCos frequently will allow a "strip" annexation only on the condition that it be greatly expanded to include unincorporated territory on both sides of the strip. Similarly, they may allow an annexation of some additional prime land on the condition that other prime land be excluded from the proposal and some less desirable land included. In addition to requiring these actual alterations, it is clear that the mere existence of LAFCos discourages the most blatant "raids."

LAFCos go about deciding whether to allow or disapprove annexation proposals, and add or subtract territory through ad hoc procedures. They weigh political factors (including the probability of electoral approval of the proposal) as well as purely economic ones.

The Folsom Example

The complexity of the problem can be suggested by an example from Sacramento.[1] Outside the City of Folsom lies an unincorporated area characterized by low density, single family detached housing. Development is spotty and the few services available are provided almost exclusively by special districts. On February 23, 1966, the Sacramento LAFCo received a request from the City of Folsom to annex a strip of business land along Main Avenue, the single major street that bisects the unincorporated area. Seventeen days later the LAFCo received a proposal to incorporate a separate City of Orangevale, which would include the same strip, plus a sizable amount of surrounding territory.

On one hand, it appeared clearly inequitable to allow the City of Folsom to drain off the area's most important tax base, because many of the stores along the main street relied on patronage by the residents

of the land proposed for incorporation into the new city.
On the other hand, even with the inclusion of the business area, the proposed City of Orangevale would lack a
tax base sufficient to make it more than "half a city."
Further, to create such a weak city government in an area
with numerous strong special districts would almost inevitably lead to conflict.

Finally, even the compromise solutions would have
created problems. Either (1) forcing the City of Folsom
to expand the area of its annexation, or (2) forcing
the proposed City of Orangevale to reduce its area of
incorporation would leave fringe areas of an exceedingly
awkward size. They would be too small either for any
likelihood of incorporation or for efficient service by
equally small special districts.

The LAFCo denied both proposals. The commission
also denied a subsequent proposal to form a much larger
new City of San Juan, with 50 square miles and 80,000
inhabitants, which would include the area proposed for
the City of Orangevale. Largely as a result of the continuing controversy over this area, the LAFCo is now con-
ducting a comprehensive study of the entire county with
the aid of a citizens' council. A final solution may
emerge from that effort.

There is no easy answer to such a complex situation, but decisions would be helped by analyzing a number of factors. For example, it would be useful to know
(1) the percentage of Orangevale residents who patronize
the Main Street shops; (2) the projected budget of the
proposed city; (3) potential tax revenue from the area;
(4) the current cost of special district government; and
(5) the way the city proposes to provide services and
phase out special districts.

CONTROLLING THE PROLIFERATION OF SPECIAL DISTRICTS

Another key function assigned to LAFCos was to
control the proliferation of independent special district

governments. The LAFCos have used a wide variety of
approaches to achieve this end, but it is disturbing to
find that the total number of special districts continued to rise by about 100 per year, even after the LAFCos
came into existence. As noted earlier, however, the
most recent statewide figures indicate that the future
will see changes. In keeping with the original intent,
LAFCos should disapprove most new formations and vigor-
ously use the District Reorganization Act to decrease
the total number of districts.

The case against special districts has been forcefully stated by a number of authors.[2] Special districts
frequently pursue their own ends, oblivious of larger
patterns of development. The fragmentation of decision
making makes it difficult if not impossible to formulate a unified, efficient policy for the provision of
governmental services. Further, residents are usually
either unaware of the existence of many districts, or
apathetic and unwilling to vote for their directors.
For those reasons, districts are essentially undemocratic institutions. Because of their low visibility
they are particularly subject to special interest manipulation or fraud.

On the other hand, the case for special districts
includes the fact that many come into existence to provide a service that other local government entities cannot, or will not deal with: sometimes because no other
appropriate governmental entity exists; sometimes because of statutory limits on debts; sometimes because
of political expediency; and sometimes because of bu-
reaucratic arteriosclerosis.

It is clear that each proposal for district formation should be considered on its merits. In certain
sparsely populated areas, special districts may be the
most rational means of providing services. Some
districts--notably water and sewer districts--should
logically be formed with respect to topography, and
not political boundaries. In addition, the argument

against fragmentation of government may be largely met by multifunctional districts that fulfill the function of coordination. If elected officials of a city or county act as the governing body of a local unit (as in the case of a county service area) the arguments citing the district's lack of visibility and undemocratic character are at least partially countered. It should be noted, however, that a county service area is not legally a special district, despite certain similarities. (See discussion in latter part of Ch. IV.)

Finally, it is important to remember that recent legislation controls the sale of certain types of district bonds and the distribution of assets upon dissolution, and makes both consolidation and dissolution of districts easier. Such changes and controls have tended to affect the character of districts and make them a "healthier" type of government than they were a few years ago.

GOVERNMENTAL MODIFICATION AND THE LAND DEVELOPERS

Land developers often make proposals for the modification of governmental structures. Some of these proposed reorganizations are logical, but in other cases the developer stands to gain and the public may lose. One aspect of the problem is, of course, related to special districts.

The Assembly Interim Committee on Municipal and County Government has conducted hearings on the use of special district government as an aid to land development.[3] The committee found that frequently small special districts are formed at the instigation of developers to provide services, and that this often in fact provides a subvention for the developer.[4] Innumerable subdivision-sized special districts have all of the worst characteristics of special districts that were noted above. LAFCos may act to prevent the formation of the land developer districts altogether, if there is an

alternative way to provide services. The commissions may
also cause County Service Areas to be formed: this type
of district is governed by the county board of supervisors (so that it is not subject to developer manipulation) and is not "splintered" off from total service
planning. Service areas also automatically dissolve upon
annexation or incorporation of the territory.

Developers often use the devices of annexation and
incorporation in much the same way as they use special
districts.[5]

As a general rule, proposals made by a single developer are closely scrutinized by LAFCos. Those that
are clearly irrational will be denied, while some that
benefit both the developer and the larger community
will be accepted. The stronger LAFCos conduct careful
inquiries and are firm in their denials; the weaker ones
are less penetrating and forceful. LAFCos have had a
salutary effect, but they could do still better.

IMPLEMENTING SOCIAL POLICIES

Implicit in many of the LAFCos' actions are attempts to achieve a more equitable distribution of costs
and benefits in order to implement broad social policies. In seeking to avoid tax base raiding, the underlying assumption is that communities accepting the
benefit of highly taxable property should also bear the
burden of providing municipal services to the residential areas.

If a city is near a tract of unincorporated land
with a factory and a large area of modest homes where
the families of the factory workers live, it may be
rational for LAFCos to make simultaneous annexation of
the area of tract homes a condition for annexing the
factory. If, in the hypothetical case, the residential
area were occupied by unemployed Chicanos, the same

decision may lack the abstract "rational" basis, but represent justifiable social policy. LAFCos have the power to structure a just system of local government, and to incorporate in their decisions the same type of moral judgments evidenced in proposals for tax sharing, welfare, and school integration.

No LAFCos articulate this moral force as official policy. For political reasons, actions which in effect benefit Negroes or Mexican-Americans are phrased in terms of economics, or design. Actions that effectively subsidize one community or subsection of a community at the expense of another are never treated in these terms.

LAFCos and Social Change

There are two types of situations in which adjacent communities are economically and ethnically separate and in which boundary change is an important tool for effectuating social change. In the first, a decaying, older core city is surrounded by new suburbs. The old core is likely to have deteriorating water and sewer mains, out-of-date lighting, a heavy demand for police protection, and structures that are potential fire hazards. To annex suburban territory that lacks these problems but has well-to-do property owners and highly taxable research and development industries, in effect constitutes a "subsidy" to the core city. Such a subsidy may be highly desirable. The core city contains facilities that benefit the entire area; in many cases suburban industries employ "reverse commuters," and the burden of upgrading living conditions for the core area ethnic minorities is an areawide problem.

The second situation is exactly the opposite. In a number of areas, existing cities have systematically annexed all of the valuable tax property from unincorporated land near them, leaving "pockets" of unincorporated land to become slums. The remaining pockets are also in need of subsidy.

North Fontana

Some examples may clarify the problem and illustrate what LAFCos can do. On the hillside above the
City of Fontana in San Bernardino County lies the North
Fontana area. It is unincorporated, populated largely
by Blacks, and is quite poor. Fontana has no desire to
annex this land. Above North Fontana is a strip of
prime land that Fontana would very much like to annex.
The LAFCo has placed a condition on the annexation of
the prime land; it is concurrent annexation of the
"problem area." The commission has looked with dis-
favor upon separate incorporation of the North Fontana
area which would "freeze" it as a ghetto.

Recently the City of Rialto annexed land which for
the first time made its boundaries contiguous to both
North Fontana and the prime land above it. Now Rialto,
too, may be interested in "skimming the cream" and
leaving North Fontana. With the rivalry between the
two cities, LAFCo is in a strong bargaining position--
it may play upon the rivalry for the choice land in
order to get one of the cities to annex all of North
Fontana, or both cities to annex portions of it. Im-
provements in the North Fontana area would come largely
from the taxes of the richer annexing communities and
from the "prime land" they would also take. This would
be a socially useful subsidization of the impoverished
area by the richer community.

East Palo Alto

A somewhat similar situation exists in San Mateo
County. East Palo Alto is a pocket of essentially
urban, but unincorporated land that has become a Black
ghetto in one of the richest counties in the United
States. It is between 55 and 65 percent Black. While
it contains only 5 percent of San Mateo's population

it contains one-third of the county's dependent population.[6] All of the standard ghetto problems are present: low incomes, high unemployment, overcrowded and substandard housing, high rates of broken families and illegitimacy, crime and juvenile delinquency.

A study of East Palo Alto was conducted by the staff of the San Mateo County LAFCo, partly in response to an annexation proposal, and partly in order to stimulate the county supervisors into making a Model Cities application to the federal Department of Housing and Urban Development. The study is significant in that it contains estimates of the comparative costs of leaving the area unincorporated, of incorporating it as a separate city, or of having it annexed to the adjacent cities of Palo Alto or Menlo Park.

The estimates indicate that leaving the area unincorporated would not be an acceptable solution, because such pockets of unincorporated urban land require urban services. Overall county services designed for rural or sparsely settled areas are simply not adequate. In addition, it is clear that other residents of the county would continue to pay a large percentage of the costs of servicing East Palo Alto.[7] It is equally clear from the East Palo Alto study that incorporation of the area would probably be financially impossible as well as undesirable.[8] Such an area cannot generate sufficient revenue on its own to finance even marginal municipal services, and its needs for services are in excess of those of wealthier neighbors.

Incorporation must of necessity freeze the area as a ghetto, woefully underfinanced, lacking the economies of scale and accumulated expertise that would result from annexation to an adjacent municipality, and permanently severed from the community of richer neighbors.

Finally, the study indicates that annexation of the area to an adjacent municipality is not a good solution.

Either the level of services of the annexing municipality must sink, or the level of services in the annexed area must be raised radically. A radical raise does two things: (1) It increases the tax rate in the annexed area--often markedly, putting greatly increased financial pressures on the demonstrably impoverished residents, perhaps cutting off a useful way station in the migration and adjustment of deprived Blacks from the rural south to western urban society; and (2) It raises the tax rate of the annexing area, often markedly.[9] As noted earlier, the annexing city is in effect subsidizing the annexed area. Local government is forced to bear the costs of a national failure; costs generated in Mississippi, Harlem, and Watts.

Federal Financing

In the light of the inadequacy of these other solutions, federal financing, particularly through the Model Cities program would seem to be the best solution. It could be provided as a subsidy to an annexing city or to a newly incorporating city. In the case of East Palo Alto the county board of supervisors was stimulated to submit to H.U.D. a Model Cities application that was denied. Perhaps acceptance of a new application will provide a solution to that area's critical problems.

IMPROVING THE PATTERN OF URBANIZATION

One of the stated objectives of the LAFCo legislation is the "discouragement of urban sprawl."[10] Construed narrowly, this would seem to be a directive only to prevent the creation of premature subdivisions and the drawing of illogical boundaries. The mandate, however, is general, and provides a rationale for many different types of LAFCo activity.

The European Approach

In England, where land is scarcer and the tradition of land use regulation more developed, the government is implementing comprehensive policies to limit the size of cities, surround them with greenbelts, and locate the overspill in new towns. Similarly stringent land use controls and planned development are common in other European countries where land is regarded as a scarce resource. In the United States generally there has been a rapidly increasing trend toward tight control, particularly in the last few years. In California, in particular, the tremendous population boom and the staggering amount of new construction, both present and planned, will almost certainly force the adoption of increasingly strict land use controls. LAFCos should have a vitally important role as this occurs.

An Optimal Size for Cities

So far, no LAFCo is yet so theoretically oriented or politically bold as to consider the systematic denial of annexations, incorporations, and new special district formations around the edges of cities so as to create greenbelts and force the overspill to locate elsewhere. Yet there are already gropings in this direction. The trend towards surveying all the land in a county and designating fixed "city spheres of influence" shows that LAFCos are beginning to give serious thought to the optimal size of cities within their jurisdictions. Furthermore, LAFCos have acted effectively to guarantee that the ideas they have formed do not remain idle speculation. Another development of great interest is the fact that LAFCos have discovered that they can be useful in preserving open space.

A conference of executive officers held at Lake Arrowhead in October 1968 devoted substantial discussion to the topic of what LAFCos can do with this problem.

The San Mateo LAFCo has drawn a sphere of influence around a large tract of undeveloped land in the middle of San Mateo County. There is consensus that it should be retained as open space, and the LAFCo indicates that it will not allow proposals that would disturb the natural condition of the area. Needless to say, it is impossible to develop an area if the LAFCo refuses to allow creation of a government to provide services to it. San Bernardino County has in some instances imposed the requirement that a multifunction district assume the responsibility for preserving open space as a precondition of the district's formation, where the authorizing legislation permits the district to exercise such power.

NOTES

CHAPTER III

1. Interview with Fred Christiansen, Sacramento LAFCo executive officer.

2. See, for example, John C. Bollens, *Special District Governments in the United States* (Berkeley: University of California Press, 1957); and Advisory Commission on Intergovernmental Relations, *A Commission Report: The Problems of Special Districts in American Government*, A-22 (Washington, D.C.: May 1964).

3. State of California, Assembly, Interim Committee Report 1961-1963 (Volume 6, Number 20) *Uses of Special Assessment Procedures and Independent Special Districts to Aid Land Development*.

4. This is not necessarily true in all cases. Many counties (particularly in rural areas) require that there be a public agency to provide essential services (such as water and sewers). In some such situations where there are no interested members of the public who can serve as officers, "developer instituted" districts are a necessity. For example, as a general rule members of the public do not clamor to contest elections of the board of directors of sewer districts.

5. Robert B. Rigney, *Opportunities, Problems and Landmark Decisions of the San Bernardino County Local Agency Formation Commission* (San Bernardino County: April 28, 1966), hereafter Rigney, *Opportunities,* reports the following example: The City of Rialto in San Bernardino County had an area of unincorporated fringe land adjacent to the city. The county had zoned the land R1 (prime residential). A developer wanted to have it zoned C2 (medium commercial) in order to put in a supermarket. When he applied to the county for a zoning change there were numerous complaints from adjacent landowners that the shopping center would be a

76

nuisance and hurt property values.   The county refused
the zoning change.

Ordinarily in such cases the developer would appeal
this decision to the county board of supervisors or to
the courts if he felt that the zoning commission had
abused its discretion. This developer adopted a more
devious strategy. He requested annexation of his land
to the City of Rialto, on the assumption that he could
get the city to zone it as he wished. His annexation
proposal was carefully trimmed to exclude dissenting
landowners. In the absence of LAFCo review the annexation would certainly have taken place. As it was the
developer faced a vigorous review with careful fact-
finding and considerable controversy.

After holding a series of hearings, the LAFCo approved a modified annexation, on condition that it include more regularly shaped boundaries and also include
many of the property owners who opposed the zoning change.
Faced with this alternative, the developer abandoned his
annexation attempt. This example is illustrative of the
way in which private developers could abuse annexation
provisions prior to LAFCo.

6. M. F. Rolih, *Staff Report to the San Mateo
County Local Agency Formation Commission: East Palo
Alto Annexation Study*, File No. 66-29 (San Mateo Coun-
ty: January 17, 1967), p. 13.

7. Ibid., Appendix G, p. 1. County expenditures
in excess of revenues derived from the area were
$343,835 in fiscal 1966-1967.

8. Ibid., Appendix G, p. 3. If East Palo Alto
were to be incorporated and if the rough estimates of
the LAFCo staff are correct, the estimated budget would
run an annual deficit of $61,000.

9. Ibid. Estimated figures in the case of East
Palo Alto are as follows. If East Palo Alto were

78

annexed to either Palo Alto or Menlo Park, the annual household increase in taxes in the richer community would run between $35 and $70 annually. But the annexation would also increase the annual household tax expense in East Palo Alto--approximately $36 per household if the LAFCo staff figures are correct.

Thus the annexation would have two different tax effects. Residents of the richer annexing community would be heavily subsidizing their poorer neighbors. The incidence of the subsidy would be highly fortuitous-- defined by lines on the map which have nothing at all to do with the causes of East Palo Alto's poverty. Of far greater concern, the tax burden on residents of East Palo Alto would skyrocket. In fiscal 1966-1967 the tax levy averaged $103.30 per household; thus the projected $36 increase would represent a very substantial rise. The effect of this increase in an area as poor as East Palo Alto might be disastrous.

10. *California Government Code* §54774.

CHAPTER IV

The Future of Urban Planning

The effectiveness of LAFCos depends to a great extent upon the quality of their planning. Unless there
is a clear idea of what type of governmental structure
is desirable, "policing" the specific proposals submitted to them has little meaning.

The statute explicitly gives LAFCos the power to
make studies, and advises them to consult existing land
use planning entities. Assemblyman John Knox has been
a forceful exponent of the view that LAFCos should use
these powers to the limit, and that each LAFCo should
formulate a "master plan" for the development of governmental services.[1]

There are three major ways in which LAFCos can plan.
First, if they write comprehensive, meaningful standards
and stick to them this activity would in effect constitute "planning." Second, they may work with existing
land use planning entities. Finally, they may do their
own "governmental services" planning. LAFCos have not
engaged in the first type of planning with great success,
but there are very interesting and encouraging developments in the other two areas.

WEAKNESS OF "STANDARDS" DEVELOPED BY LAFCOS

§54774 of the *California Government Code* specifically authorizes LAFCos to make studies and gives them
permission to ask for information from other existing
planning entities. The paragraph states:

> One of the objects of the local agency
> formation commission is to make studies
> and to obtain and furnish information
> which will contribute to the logical
> and reasonable development of local
> governments.... Such studies may in-
> clude, but shall not be limited to
> inventorying such agencies and deter-
> mining their maximum service area and
> service capacities...the commission
> may ask for land use information, stud-
> ies, and plans of cities, counties,
> and districts...and may cooperate with
> the county planning commissions.

The precise nature of LAFCo studies is not spelled out,
nor is there any definition of the "cooperation" with
other planning entities that is called for.

Among factors LAFCos "shall" consider in reviewing
any proposal are several that look to the future. A
pertinent part of §54796 provides:

> Factors to be considered in the review
> of a proposal shall include, but not be
> limited to:
>
> (a) Population, population density;
> land area and land use; per capita
> assessed valuation; topography, natu-
> ral boundaries, and drainage basins;
> proximity to other populated areas;
> the likelihood of significant growth
> in the area, and in adjacent incor-
> porated and unincorporated areas
> during the next ten years.

(b) Need for organized community services; the present cost and adequacy of governmental services and controls in the area; probable future needs for such services and controls; probable effect of the proposed incorporation, formation, annexation, or exclusion and of alternative courses of action on the cost and adequacy of services and controls in the area and adjacent areas.

(c) The effect of the proposed action and of alternative actions, on adjacent areas, on mutual social and economic interests and on the local governmental structure of the county.

This section provides essential minima that must be considered, but does not provide adequate criteria for decision making. It attaches no weight to the list of "factors to be considered," and makes no claim to completeness. No clear connections are made between these factors and the general goals--such as discouraging urban sprawl--which are spelled out elsewhere in the law. Thus the section provides a framework, but leaves much to the imagination, judgment, and fortitude of the individual executive officer. Phrases such as need for organized community services, or their present adequacy or the likelihood of significant growth, by their very nature suggest the need for careful interpretation.

In order to fill in these gaps the drafters of the LAFCo legislation expected that each LAFCo would develop its own set of standards. §54790(b) of the *Government Code* specifically gives them the power: "To adopt standards and procedures for the evaluation of proposals."

The hopes of the drafters have not been met. Today most LAFCos have not adopted formal standards. Some have explicitly decided not to adopt standards;

some are delaying, until they have a clearer idea of
what such standards should contain.

The Ventura County Survey

In August 1966, Ventura County conducted a survey
of LAFCos to determine what standards had been developed.[2] Those submitted ranged from a one page "check-
list" prepared by Orange County (which merely restates
the exact words of the *Government Code* §54796), to a
fairly wordy (if not helpful) set submitted by Los
Angeles County.

Perhaps the standards of Marin County were the
most useful. The heart of the Marin County standards
is a set of priorities:

> (6) New or consolidated service
> should be provided by one of
> the following governmental
> agencies in the descending
> order of preference:
>
> (a) Annexation to an existing
> city.
> (b) Annexation to an existing
> district of which the Board
> of Supervisors is the governing
> body.
> (c) Annexation to an existing
> multiple purpose special
> district.
> (d) Annexation to another existing
> district.
> (e) A new county service area.
> (f) Incorporation of a new city.
> (g) Formation of a new multiple
> purpose district.
> (h) Formation of a new single pur-
> pose district.[3]

These standards embody a set of values generally shared, if not articulated, by most LAFCos. The statement presents a definite policy and is of some use in informing advocates of their chances for success, but it is much too brief to provide effective guidance. Arguably, a similar type of guideline, developed in greater detail, would come closer to the goal of providing a plan.

Most other existing standards are gobbledygook: useless as aids to decision making, confusing rather than helpful to proponents, and filed and forgotten in the best interests of all concerned.

Are Standards Needed?

Why have LAFCos not articulated specific standards? An important reason is that their goals and strategies are changing rapidly and many do not want to risk becoming too firmly set too soon. Another important reason is that most decisions are routine and do not require the application of standards. In addition, the decisions/are often complex and highly political and LAFCo members do not want to be bound by fixed rules. Finally, in most counties a small circle of well-informed politicians, consultants, and attorneys is developing, persons who are familiar with LAFCo operations. Their presence often makes brief written standards superfluous.

A more important question is whether the lack of written standards really matters. The answer depends to a large extent on two other questions that will be answered in the succeeding sections of this chapter: How do LAFCos and planning departments relate to each other? and What "plans" are LAFCos making? If LAFCos were not planning effectively in other ways, the absence of unequivocal standards would constitute a serious dereliction of duty. However, because LAFCos are doing more and more serious planning, the absence of guidelines is of much less consequence. In this situation, "planning" serves much the same function as the adoption of standards.

COOPERATING WITH LAND USE PLANNERS

§54774 of the *Government Code* originally authorized LAFCos to "ask for land use information, studies, and plans of cities and counties...and [to] cooperate with the county planning commission." In 1967 an amendment included special district studies. To what extent have LAFCos complied? One of the major purposes of the LAFCos study, conducted under the auspices of the Intergovernmental Council on Urban Growth, was to answer that question. The findings stated:

> ...LAFCos generally use them [general plans] where they exist, and to the extent that their nature permits. Executive officers, particularly, welcome guides of this sort, which can substantiate LAFC decisions and also afford a means of placing many otherwise routine, almost meaningless, small city and district annexation proposals in a broader context.[4]

By a 1967 amendment to the LAFCo legislation, LAFCos are explicitly prevented from attaching conditions regarding land use or subdivision standards to city annexation proposals. Nonetheless the effect of LAFCo decisions on land use is evident. If, for example, a LAFCo will not approve extension of a water district's jurisdiction to a new subdivision, the commission can effectively kill a projected development. Conversely, a local planning agency may refuse to rezone land and thus cripple the effectiveness of a proposed LAFCo action. Clearly the two entities should be working closely together.

Existing city and county general plans are usually inadequate in that they do not contain concrete proposals for moving from existing conditions to the desired end-state they project. To make such plans useful, it is necessary to coordinate existing governmental powers and direct them towards fulfilling planned goals: zoning, subdivision control, capital improvement programs, regulations under the police power, nuisance law--all can be effective devices for implementing a general plan. If the considerable power of a LAFCo is added, a significant step will have been taken toward the creation of viable plans.

In addition to using existing plans, there are a number of ways in which LAFCos interact with planning agencies. Frequently LAFCo proposals are sent to county or city planning bodies for review and suggestions. In some cases there are regular prehearing meetings between the LAFCo executive officer and other concerned agencies, including planning personnel. In 31 counties there is such a review; in 26 there is none. In Orange, Merced, and Napa counties a member of the county planning office serves as the LAFCo executive officer.[5]

DEVELOPING RESEARCH AND PROVIDING INFORMATION

§54774 of the *Government Code* states that:

> One of the objects of the local agency
> formation commission is to make studies
> and to obtain and furnish information
> which will contribute to the logical
> and reasonable development of local
> governments.....

Thus the instruction to "obtain and furnish information" spells out two sorts of activities for the LAFCos: (1) to obtain information that may be of use to them in their work, and (2) to act as clearinghouses to provide information to others. In pursuit of these aims, LAFCo executive officers frequently comment that for the first time they are succeeding in bringing conflicting entities together to talk with each other and to consider larger areawide interests.

Technical Studies and Philosophic Problems

A number of the studies may be considered to be purely technical, or "inventory" studies, for example that of San Bernardino County which produced a series of transparent overlays showing the existing locations of various facilities and jurisdictions.

Of considerably greater interest is the growing number of studies that go beyond inventories, studies of purely technical problems, or a focus on a single controversy. They consider more general questions about what the governmental structure should be. Some have been aimed at special district reorganizations such as fire districts (in Sacramento County), or lighting districts (in Ventura County); several sought comprehensive solutions for the problems of populous unincorporated areas;[6] one attempted to find a formula for tax sharing between a county and a city after an important annexation;[7] and one examined the expansion of a harbor district (in Ventura County).

In addition there are the important "city sphere of influence" studies, which will be discussed in detail in the next section. Finally, two current long-range, planning studies merit particular comment: San Diego's Upper San Diego River Basin Pilot Study, and Sacramento County's Advisory Council Study.[8]

The San Diego Study

The Upper San Diego River Basin Pilot Study concentrates on a single small (but governmentally complex) area in order to create a procedure in which LAFCo, the county planning department, and an ad hoc special district advisory committee can effectively cooperate. If city-county-special district-LAFCo coordination can be achieved there, the implication is that it can be achieved elsewhere in the county. It is still too early to tell what will happen, or to what extent it will be possible to transfer insights gained in that operation to countywide planning; but this is an interesting and significant experiment that should have implications beyond San Diego County.

The Sacramento Study

Partly as a result of the Folsom-Orangevale-San Juan conflict discussed in Chapter III, Sacramento has established a 30-member, countywide advisory council to devise an action program for governmental development through 1980. Whether the 30 members (6 from governmental bodies; 12 from regions of the county; and 12 representing a cross-section of community leadership) will be able to agree on a report; what the report will contain; and how effectively it can be implemented are all matters of conjecture at this time. Here, as in San Diego, one can perceive the beginning of new developments.

CITY SPHERES OF INFLUENCE

While "planning through the use of standards" has not occurred, the two foregoing sections demonstrate that LAFCos have construed the general mandate to make studies and to cooperate with existing planning entities in such a way that they are increasingly discharging planning functions. This trend is illustrated even more clearly in the increasing use of city spheres of influence and the studies used to determine their boundaries.

San Bernardino County

The reasons for city spheres may be illustrated by the situation in San Bernardino County.[9] Between Montclair, Chino, and Ontario lay a five to six mile area of unincorporated territory. It was served by a jumble of special districts and, as is characteristic of unincorporated land, had a level of municipal service lower than that of the surrounding cities. Because of the rate of growth in the area, it was clear that eventually the entire area would be urbanized and incorporated.

Each city saw its own interest in annexing as much of the area as possible; and each realized that the other two cities had the same designs. All three were moving to preempt land they felt they might ultimately want. (This is a pure example of the type of annexation war that has long been common in California, particularly in areas of rapid urbanization, and most notably in Santa Clara County.)

Complexities may be introduced in such a situation by increasing the number of actors, reducing the certainty of ultimate total annexation, and increasing the tangle of special districts. In some areas where cities have already included land outside their boundaries in city general plans, or have prezoned it, or have extended some services on a temporary basis under contract, decisions may be even more complex. The following model case well illustrates the forces that tend to make development irrational.

Chino, fearing that Ontario might move to annex some contested land, was making plans to move prematurely to take a piece of that rural land itself. If the area should be incorporated into the City of Chino, municipal services of the same level as provided elsewhere in Chino could only be provided at great expense and with considerable waste.

In this situation, the San Bernardino LAFCo took strong action. When the next proposal for a minor annexation was made, the LAFCo denied it and suggested to the mayors of the three cities (Chino, Montclair, and Ontario) that they get together and agree on the ultimate boundaries of their cities before the LAFCo took any further action.

The mayors did meet (in a public hearing), but were unable to solve the problem. They decided to refer the matter to a committee composed of their planning directors, a representative from the county planning department, and the LAFCo staff. The planning directors met, but could not agree.

At this stage, the LAFCo staff made a study and prepared a report that was adopted as official LAFCo policy and was made public. Since that time, all LAFCo decisions in the area have been in conformity with the report.

It is possible to say that such a procedure allows development that is rational in a number of senses. The cities cease premature preemptive annexations, and instead take only land that has developed enough so that annexation makes sense. The LAFCo, having outlined ultimate city boundaries, will allow some irregularly shaped annexations in the expectation that they will ultimately be part of a regular set of boundaries, thus facilitating development. The report has been made explicit "policy" and therefore retains the requisite mixture of flexibility and authoritativeness.

This is not a very dramatic or unusual example of the delineation of a city sphere. It does, however, illustrate the nature of the problem. After a description of some of the other counties in which city spheres are being used, it will be useful to return to this example and point out some features that make it particularly significant.

Ventura County

Ventura County has gone further than any other county in California in setting out city spheres of influence. Its city sphere study in fact represents a general plan for the county, which is similar to city general plans. The Ventura LAFCo has created city spheres that cover all the present and potential urban areas of the county, looking ahead to the year 2000.[10] The study also outlines the boundaries of four new cities that should be incorporated in the future, but are not now in existence. One point of particular controversy in the plan was the incorporation of the new City of Los Posas in the Los Posas Valley between the large, aggressively annexing cities of Oxnard and Camarillo. Both of these cities had designs on the Los Posas Valley area. The LAFCo has since backed down and agreed that the area will be split between the two cities.

Any plan as far-ranging and general as that of Ventura County poses difficult problems. For example, conditions may change in such a way as to make long-range plans obsolete. There are, however, factors that make Ventura a uniquely appropriate county for such general planning: (1) The great wave of urbanization in Southern California is just beginning to move into Ventura County. (2) Ventura has a relatively uncomplicated local government structure. (3) Of even greater importance is the fact that strong topographical features (mountains and valleys) dictate many boundary choices.

On the other hand, these facts suggest that counties with different characteristics may not be suitable bases for long-range plans. For example, counties with complex governmental structures, where urbanization is well underway, and where there are no strong topographical features, may be ill-advised to draw up a long-range and general document.

Other counties are working out other city spheres of influence. In addition to the Montclair-Chino-Ontario sphere noted, San Bernardino County has sketched out seven other spheres of influence. The San Mateo County LAFCo has conducted hearings in each city in the county to determine ultimate city spheres.

Some counties have explicitly decided not to adopt city spheres of influence, notably Los Angeles and San Diego. However, both these counties do encourage cities to work out their own agreements.

Technical and Political Decisions

Assuming that city spheres of some kind should be created, the really difficult questions are those relating to procedure, form, and degree. How should spheres be created? By whom? With what enforcement mechanisms and what degree of flexibility?

On one hand, it is possible to imagine city agreements worked out without any LAFCo participation.[11] On the other hand, there could be spheres unilaterally dictated by LAFCos. In between, there are varying degrees and forms of consultation and firmness.

For political reasons, it is difficult for mayors or city councilmen to agree upon any final settlement of boundaries. In the example of the three cities in San Bernardino County, the mayors met in a public hearing where it would have been politically embarrassing to agree that any land in controversy was not within their own spheres. The referral of the problem to the planning officials of the cities shows the mayors' desire to have the decision grounded in technical considerations that would lessen the political heat. However, local planners are attuned to local political realities, and there are similar pressures on them not to "give away" potentially claimable territory. It is also difficult for a planner to make a "technical" decision against the political interests of the community.

In a situation such as this, the intervention of an outside arbiter is welcomed by all parties, because it relieves political pressure. LAFCos provide a forum in which difficult decisions can be made by officials who are not in danger of losing the next election as a result.

If the LAFCo will ultimately make the final decision, one wonders why it should not do so in the first place without going through the ritual of routing it through mayors and planners. There are several reasons for taking the long way. First, the process of moving a question through mayors and planners and then back to the LAFCo generates data, not merely technical data, but also information on what the involved parties perceive their respective interests to be. This minimizes the danger of serious LAFCo error.

Second, the ritual places LAFCo in the correct role. It is ultimately firm, but is not remote, dictatorial, or unsympathetic to local views. When decisions are reached in this way, they are easier for the cities to accept. Robert Rigney, the San Bernardino LAFCo executive officer, perceptively summarized the process as follows:

> It would appear that the cities in controversy cannot back down on their own initiative for civic pride or political reasons, but they have accepted the decisions of the local agency formation commission as an outside arbiter with good grace.[12]

The Nature of the Plans

Another general problem is how specific such plans should be. How long range? How flexible? Ventura's sweeping long-range planning is in sharp contrast to San Bernardino's approach, which defers decisions until conflict is imminent. There is no right answer to such a problem. As suggested earlier, the radically different topographies and the degrees of urbanization of the two counties go far towards justifying the two different

approaches. Their experience suggests that other counties should avoid adopting models borrowed uncritically
from their neighbors.

The Noncity Problem

One specific problem related to city spheres of
influence is the case in which there may be a city organized some time in the future, but where development
has not proceeded to the point that a new incorporation
is presently justifiable. San Bernardino has run into
trouble in the Cucamonga area; Ventura, particularly in
the Los Posas Valley. Where unincorporated land has
been put into the sphere of an existing city and re-
quests (1) annexation to another city, or (2) incorporation, or (3) formation of a powerful multifunctional
special district, the LAFCo can turn down the request
in good conscience and explain that it considers annexation to the existing city more logical. Where the LAFCo
has placed a piece of unincorporated land in the
sphere of a noncity it cannot make that argument. In
such a situation, a county service area may be the answer.

Criteria

Criteria that are used in determining city spheres
of influence vary widely. All of the factors set out
in the *Government Code* as guides to all LAFCo decision
making are relevant. As noted above, topography was
the dominant consideration in Ventura County. San
Mateo set out a number of considerations and suggested
that cities submitting proposals "...be as explicit
as possible in arriving at cost benefit ratios and
the like."[13]

There is some interesting evidence that the pref-
erence of inhabitants may depend on subtle considerations. Several counties have discovered that residents

of an area will consider themselves part of the community in whose postal zone they live.[14] Because their
mail comes with a community name on it, they feel they
belong in that community. To a lesser extent this
is true also of school districts. One city sphere study
went beyond balancing economic and engineering considerations and actually polled residents of an area in question. Twenty-six hundred residents of the unincorporated
area between the cities of Fontana and Rialto in San
Bernardino County were polled. Each resident was provided with brief, explicit statements by both cities and
the county explaining the relative merits of annexing to
one or the other or of remaining unincorporated. The
poll results in this instance did not prove to be very
helpful because respondents appeared to misunderstand the
information provided.[15]

INTERIM STRATEGIES ON THE URBAN FRINGE: COUNTY SERVICE AREAS

The bulk of LAFCo problems occur in dealing with
the fringe areas around existing cities. This is where
most development is taking place and where various
types of conflicts are most likely to occur. Once a
LAFCo has a clear idea of the direction of future development, it is possible to plan ways of servicing
this area so that other arrangements can be devised in
the future. At every stage of development an appropriate governmental structure is needed. A fully urbanized area should have a city government, but there
should be no premature annexations or incorporations.
In the interim, a way should be found to provide an
appropriate level of service somewhat lower than that
of a city. LAFCos continuously face the unresolved
problem of interim governmental arrangements.

In the fall of 1967 the jurisdiction of LAFCos was
extended to include review of proposals for the formation of new county service areas. County service areas
have a number of characteristics that make them particularly useful transition entities for urban fringes.

Their powers may range from a single very limited function (most commonly the provision of street lighting) to a cluster of functions almost as great as that of a city (other than land use regulation powers).

The fact that they are governed by the county board of supervisors prevents the worst inefficiency and myopia which are characteristic of urban fringe districts. Of even greater importance, any territory is automatically dropped from a county service area when it becomes part of a city. In §25210.90, the *California Government Code* provides:

> Whenever any territory in a county service area is included within a city by reason of incorporation, annexation or otherwise that territory shall be automatically excluded from the county service area upon the effective date of its inclusion in the city.... Upon the exclusion of such territory all unencumbered funds standing to the credit of the area upon the date of the exclusion shall be divided between the city and the county service area in proportion to the assessed value of the real property of the territory excluded and the portion remaining.

Thus county service areas are flexible entities that may provide any of a variety of services, that keep control from being fragmented among many independent districts, and that automatically disappear with annexation or incorporation. In San Bernardino County, 64 county service areas have been created--frequently in fringe areas. It is an indication of the utility of such districts in the fringe situation that only 33 still exist. Many of the others have been absorbed.

In opposing such use of county service areas it is sometimes argued that the provision of so many services

may discourage annexations and freeze the level of services at a low level, without municipal land use controls
(although county zoning still prevails), and with authority removed from the locality and vested in the county.

The answer would appear to be that in most instances,
as urbanization proceeds and new services are added, the
rising costs will push county service areas into cities.
Economies of scale, the need for greater land use controls, a desire to share in the state gas tax subvention
that goes to cities, and the wish for more local control
will push these areas into cities when they are ripe for
annexation.

There is another important emerging strategy for
dealing with the urban fringe situation. Previously,
the competition for annexation made it difficult for a
city to extend municipal services to a fringe area under contract, because of uncertainty as to who would
ultimately annex the land. The combination of LAFCo
designation of a city sphere of influence and extension
of services by contract now make it possible for a city
to maintain a stable dependent fringe, with appropriate
extension of services as the area gradually urbanizes.

NOTES

CHAPTER IV

1. Speech to LAFCo executive officer's conference, Ojai, California, Autumn 1967.

2. Memo: "Standards and Criteria for Evaluating Proposals," Ventura County LAFC, August 9, 1966.

3. Marin County LAFCo, "Guidelines for Evaluation of Proposals," adopted December 7, 1964.

4. I.C.U.G. Study, p. 20.

5. Ibid., pp. 36-37.

6. Three important examples are:
   (a) Los Angeles' long study of the Dominguez-Carson area. Summarized in Memo "From: LAFCo executive officer, To: Commission Members, Subject: Dominguez-Carson Area Information, March 6, 1967."
   (b) Sacramento's study of the controversy centering around Folsom and the proposed cities of "Orangevale" and "San Juan."
   (c) The continuing studies of the East Palo Alto area by the San Mateo LAFCo which have resulted in two Model Cities applications to H.U.D.

7. Rigney, *Opportunities*, pp. 11-16.

8. Descriptions of the projects are contained in memos to the commission from the staffs of the two counties on November 14, 1967, and on May 9, 1967 respectively.

9. Rigney, *Opportunities*, pp. 5-10.

10. Information on Ventura's city spheres of influence is contained in three documents: "Proposed City Spheres of Influence" (June 1967); Memo: "City Spheres of Influence" (November 3, 1967); and Memo: "City Spheres of Influence" (January 3, 1968). The first document was issued by the Ventura County LAFCo and the Ventura County Planning Department; the last two were issued by the LAFCo alone.

11. John A. Rehfuss, Department of Political Science, San Jose State College, is an authority on such agreements. See, for example, his article "Boundary Agreements--A Solution to the Annexation Struggle?" *Public Affairs Report*, 8 (3) (June 1967). Bulletin of the Institute of Governmental Studies, University of California, Berkeley.

12. *The First 500*, p. 49.

13. Letter of San Mateo LAFCo to concerned parties. November 2, 1967.

14. Both Robert Asbell of the Ventura LAFCo, and Robert Rigney of the San Bernardino LAFCo made this observation independently in the course of discussions with the author. In the San Bernardino County situation this "community identity" based on postal zones occurs even in sparsely populated desert areas.

15. Despite explicit statements to the pollees that the tax rate of the area would be higher in the event of annexation to Fontana, a majority of those polled indicated that they favored such a move, and checked as the reason "because the tax rate would be lower." The moral would seem to be that too much reliance on such polls is unwise. A clear, very simple poll, particularly if taken during a time of specific controversy might be helpful.

CHAPTER V

A Legislative Course for Future LAFCo Development

The LAFCo legislation as it was passed in 1963 was decidedly openended. By creating a new entity with substantial powers and relatively little statutory guidance, the Knox-Nisbet Act provided an experimental situation. In the future, as LAFCos develop their strategies and as the pressures for more rational control of governmental structure increase, there will almost certainly be modifications in the statute.

It has already been modified in two ways. (1) A series of bills have cleared up ambiguities and made minor changes. (2) In addition there have been two substantial extensions of LAFCo authority--most notably the District Reorganization Act of 1965 and the inclusion of county service areas under LAFCos' authority in 1967.

Since it is highly probable that powers will be added to LAFCos at irregular intervals during the next decade, this chapter makes some suggestions on a desirable future course for LAFCo legislation. Some legislation is long overdue, such as reform of the statutes on annexation. In addition, legislation is needed to

permit correction of confused boundaries such as pockets of unincorporated land within cities.

More wide-ranging suggestions are under consideration; particularly a "latent powers" bill that would
allow LAFCos review of all expansions of special district powers, and a "City Reorganization Act" along the
lines of the District Reorganization Act. The observations on planning have not been discussed elsewhere, and
are largely the product of the analysis described in
Chapter IV. The suggestion for creation of a state-level
review board holds little hope for immediate implementa-
tion, at least in California, although strong arguments
favoring such a board may stimulate its creation some
time in the future. Such discussion may redirect other
states (who now wish to create LAFCo-like arrangements)
to consider the state-level structure.

HELPING TO RATIONALIZE BOUNDARIES

Informed opinion in California is virtually unani-
mous in holding that certain types of city boundaries
are irrational and wasteful. These pockets, cherry
stems, corridors and the like and the reasons for
their irrationality have been mentioned in Chapter I
and Chapter III. The existence of LAFCos may deter the
creation of such configurations in the future.

Arguments for their prevention should be equally
persuasive in establishing some mechanism for eliminating existing anachronistic, annoying boundary deviations.
This has been a continuing theme in testimony given before the Assembly Committee on Municipal and County Government throughout the last decade and a half.[1]

Resistance to Change

Such anachronisms are not likely to disappear unless there is affirmative intervention to bring about

change. The handful of residents of an existing pocket will usually resist an annexation because it probably will increase their taxes. The costs generated by the inefficiency of county services are absorbed by residents of the entire county, so that the impact on residents of the pocket is not very great. Similarly the few storeowners in a strip or cherry stem area will not vote for detachment of their land from a city if it will mean subsequent incorporation in a different city with higher taxes.

One way of correcting the problem might be through changing assessment practices: if, for example, the residents of a pocket were charged the full amount it really costs the county to service them they might be forced to accept annexation to the surrounding city.

The most promising approach, however, would seem to be some sort of arrangement utilizing LAFCos, which have the most information and expertise in matters relating to governmental structure change.

The Need for LAFCo Review

In the past, bills to allow unilateral annexations of pockets without the approval of resident voters or unilateral detachment of odd-shaped projections have been defeated with the argument that it is undemocratic to compel such a reorganization without the consent of the residents. This argument overlooks the fact that pockets ordinarily benefit a very few people at the expense of other city or county taxpayers. Projections similarly benefit the few residents in the projection at the expense of those in the unincorporated area surrounding them. To allow these parasitic entities to perpetuate themselves without review by LAFCos (which are composed of elected representatives of the majority of voters in the county and its cities) is the essence of elitism.

Clearly some form of legislation is needed to permit affirmative action eliminating these annoying little
problem areas. LAFCos are the logical entities to be
entrusted with this power.

THE LOGIC OF A CITY REORGANIZATION ACT

The first step towards allowing LAFCos to modify
existing governmental structures (rather than acting
solely prospectively) was taken with respect to districts in the District Reorganization Act of 1965. Double taxation, the retention of moribund districts, and
glaringly irrational arrangements for the provision of
various services made it clear that special districts
required reorganization. Similarly, the logic and as-
sumptions underlying that act suggest that parallel
legislation should permit reorganization of cities. In
the older, urban counties where cities are already contiguous throughout the entire county, various types of
reorganization are needed now. With increasing urbanization, more incorporations, and accelerated change, it
is probable that city boundaries in many areas will require review in the future.

Without working out its contents in detail, it may
be useful to outline the general thrust of such a statute and to cite a model. The District Reorganization
Act of 1965 provided for change to be initiated relatively easily either by petition of the residents affected, or through the adoption by a legislative body
of an appropriate ordinance, resolution or order. The
proposal may be referred first to a reorganization committee; the LAFCo is then requested to make a determination on the proposed change. In most cases, elections are required; in others, the commission's decision is final.

Some such pattern could be applied in an act concerned with the reorganization of city boundaries. If,
because of an unanticipated pattern of growth city

boundaries become obsolete, it should be possible for
residents to call this fact to the attention of their
LAFCo, have the problem studied and analyzed by the officials concerned and then after open hearings, receive
a final determination on the merits of their case, without the necessity for a public vote.

Reform of the existing annexation laws should also
be included in any legislation aimed at changing the
law relating to city boundaries. The existing annexation laws are clumsy, to say the least. There are two
separate acts, one for inhabited territory[2] and one for
uninhabited territory.[3] Annexation of any area containing 12 or more residents requires a protracted and
expensive election procedure. As a result, annexation
has never been able to keep pace with actual fringe
growth, and boundaries are gerrymandered to avoid the
"inhabited" category or to pack the area of a proposed
annexation with enough favorable voters to guarantee
the success of the election.

REVIEW OF SPECIAL DISTRICT LATENT POWERS

A proposal is now under discussion to allow LFACos
to review the latent powers of all special districts.
Many special districts in California are entitled to
act as multifunctional entities. When such a district
is formed for the purpose of exercising only part of
its possible powers, those powers remaining are said
to be latent.

Assume that a LAFCo receives a proposal for the
formation of a Municipal Utility District and that the
proponents intend, initially, to use its powers only
to provide water. The *California Public Utilities Code*
§12801 provides:

>A district may acquire, construct, own,
>operate, control or use...works for
>supplying the inhabitants...with light,

> water, power, heat, transportation,
> telephone service, or other means
> of communication, or means for the
> collection, treatment or disposition
> of garbage, sewage, or refuse matter....

Assume further that lighting and sewage districts already exist in the area. In such a situation the LAFCo
staff may well reason that the proposed district is the
logical entity to provide water; but that if it branches
out to provide lighting and sewer services as well,
chaos will result: double taxation, conflicts of jurisdiction, lawsuits and no possibility for orderly provision of services on the part of any of the districts.
In such a situation the LAFCo faces a dilemma. It may
allow the formation of the district (and risk subsequent expansion that may block "orderly" development),
or it may deny the formation (despite the fact that it
is the most efficient way of providing a needed service).
The critical question is whether the LAFCo can take a
compromise position and allow the formation of the district, with the condition that its activity be limited
to the single function (in this case, water). The idea
behind the latent powers bill is to grant LAFCos this
authority with subsequent review of exercises of latent
powers.

Several LAFCos have attempted to make the limitation
of latent functions a condition of the formation of such
a district in just this way. San Diego has allowed the
formation of six community service districts (which are
all multifunctional), with conditions.[4] For example,
the Canebrake County Water District operates under this
provision:

> ...on the condition that the present
> powers of the district be limited to
> water supply and distribution and that
> any expansion of the district's power
> be subject to review and approval of
> this commission.

In San Diego there has been no conflict between the
LAFCo and any of the districts thus conditioned so far.

The San Luis Obispo Challenge

However, in San Luis Obispo County a similar condition was imposed on a community services district and
conflict did develop. The San Luis Obispo LAFCo allowed
the formation of the Cambria Community Services District,
and limited it solely to providing a sewage disposal
system.[5] After the district was formed, it proceeded
to call an election to expand the district's powers to
include all of the enumerated powers of a community services district in defiance of the LAFCo. The San Luis
Obispo district attorney submitted an opinion that:

> A community services district may
> utilize the procedure set forth in
> *Government Code* §61601 to expand its
> powers without approval of the local
> agency formation commission irrespec-
> tive of the fact that it was formed
> for the performance of a limited
> service.[6]

A latent powers bill could avoid the difficulties
brought on by such an interpretation. The bill could
be designed to give LAFCos review over any new services,
the extension of existing services, or their withdrawal,
so as to insure the existence of some entity to provide a needed service, but to exclude duplication. It
could further guarantee that any extension of existing
services would be made only with some consideration of
areawide interests.

The difficulties of translating these desirable
objectives into a workable system are considerable. At
least one LAFCo (in San Bernardino) has debated the proposal and concluded that while the objective is commend-
able it is impossible to work out a system for its im-
plementation.

Some Critical Problem Areas

Without probing too deeply, it may be important here to delineate some of the critical problem areas including: (1) the definition of what constitutes a significant extension or withdrawal of services; and (2) the definition of exactly when a district is adding a new function. There is a critical tension between the wish to give LAFCos real review functions and the need to keep them free from an administratively unrealistic workload and excessive tampering with special districts, which would create constant friction and ill-will.

(3) Enforcement will also be a problem. When a district wants to withdraw from a given service, the courts would be reluctant to attempt to enforce the continuance of the function because of the difficulties of supervising day-to-day operations to see that they were correctly carried out. If a district wants to add a function or to expand an existing one, a court would be more willing to apply the remedy of injunction to prevent that occurrence. (4) Complex provisions concerning the transfer of property owned, or spheres of control will have to be worked out.

Whether or not a latent powers bill can be written tightly enough to avoid these problems and whether it can then be applied by LAFCos with a minimum of abrasiveness are questions that cannot be answered at this time.

EXPANDING THE LAFCO PLANNING FUNCTION

Throughout this monograph, there has been an emphasis on the planning function of LAFCos, perhaps to the extent of distorting the picture of their day-to-day operations. Nonetheless, as a LAFCo activity, planning is already important, and it should become increasingly so in the future. As indicated in Ch. IV,

there are many ways in which LAFCos' "governmental services planning" can be expanded and integrated with land
use planning. The impetus might come from new legislation or from increased recognition of the vital function
it performs.

Planning could be enhanced in five major ways. (1)
If LAFCos developed more meaningful standards and ad-
hered to them, the result would be a form of planning.
This development is not taking place now, although it
is conceivable that it could occur in the future. Such
LAFCo standards need not be stated as rules; indeed a
series of reports with the high level of quality and
comprehensiveness of Robert Rigney's *The First 500* study
would accomplish the same purpose. It should be noted
that while LAFCos were explicitly empowered to do this
type of "standards" planning, most have not done so.

(2) LAFCos could be given express permission, or
even required to create a separate governmental services master plan, to be prepared in conjunction with
existing planning entities and land use plans.

(3) Informal coalitions could be formed. An example is the one San Diego County put together to study
the Upper San Diego River Basin; another is the Sacramento group organized for studying the whole county.
(4) The Santa Barbara County structure is also worthy
of mention: one person serves as LAFCo executive officer,
land development coordinator, special district coordinator, and as a member of the area planning council.
(The area planning council is the county regional planning body, established as required by the U.S. Department
of Housing and Urban Development for handling federal
funds.)

(5) The use of computer techniques may become an
important aid for LAFCos' planning. The techniques
developed for defense and business operations are
increasingly being used in land use and budget planning

at the local level, and will inevitably be used by
LAFCos. Typical LAFCo decisions involve the weighing
of complex variables. In many of the day-to-day decisions an element of imprecision does not matter, but in
the difficult cases, precise computer analysis could
provide significant help. Examples include both incorporations or large conflicting annexations, such as
East Palo Alto in San Mateo County, Folsom/Orangevale
in Sacramento County, and Dominguez/Carson in Los Angeles
County.

A STATE-LEVEL REVIEW BOARD

The increased use of data processing techniques may
also bolster the case for a state-level review board.
Such a board could maintain a staff that is conversant
with the new techniques of data manipulation, while a
shortage of qualified personnel would make it unlikely
that comparable staffs could be provided in every county in the near future. The state-level staff could handle the most difficult cases, and develop methods that
could then be transferred for use at the county level.

On the other hand, the state-level board has neither a long history of support nor evidence of current
demand. In fact, the record of CSAC opposition to the
Knox-Nisbet Act, and the strength of the home rule
forces as shown during the protracted debates, strongly
suggest that establishing a state-level board in California would be infeasible for some time to come. However, political orthodoxy is not synonymous with rationality, the climate of opinion is not static, and other
states probably will create institutions in the near future, designed to perform the same function that LAFCos
now perform in California. For these reasons, it is
worth arguing the case for a state-level review board
with some vigor.

The Function of a State Board

The approach would be to leave the existing LAFCo apparatus intact. All proposals except those involving more than one county would originally be heard and decided by the local LAFCo. A small state-level board would be created to decide multicounty cases, as well as those of sufficient import, complexity, or novelty to warrant review. Presumably, details such as the exact procedure for selecting a commission, staffing, frequency of meetings, notice, recording findings and the like could be worked out. LAFCo executive officers and commission members would always be the finders of fact in the first instance and could be given the right to argue their views before the state board.

It could easily be specified that the state board would have discretion to hear only those cases it considered sufficiently important. This would provide an automatic guarantee of a manageable caseload. Quantitative material in Chapter II indicates that only a small percentage of proposals are of the type that would be controversial enough to merit appeal.[7]

Many of the larger special districts cross a number of county lines, particularly the water, irrigation, and sanitation districts created to fit the topographical contours of an area rather than political lines. A state-level entity is needed to mediate between LAFCos in deciding proposals that cross one or more county lines.

Cross-county annexation is apparently not permitted by California law; the one decided case, *The County of San Mateo v. Palo Alto* 168 C.A. 2d (1959), so held. However, the current growth of large conurbations, particularly in the Bay Area and along the coast in Southern California make the limitations on cross-county annexation appear increasingly irrational. A recent study entitled *Cross-County Annexation by Municipal Corporations in California*[8] concludes that merely a change of the annexation laws, not a constitutional amendment, is required and forcefully argues that such legislation should be passed in California. If this is done, and it seems probable that it will be done, a similar argument can be made in favor of a state-level agency to watch over cross-county city annexations.

Political Support for a Review Board

As noted above, the immediate prospects for such a review board in California are indeed slim, but it is important to observe a paradox that suggests how a new political coalition might be forged to back such a proposal. The liberal reformers who initiated the LAFCo legislation favored a state-level commission. It is almost certain that these forces could be mobilized in favor of a state-level review board for much the same reasons: it would have a broader perspective on policy, better staff, and a view less parochial and freer from local politics.

On the other end of the spectrum, the more conservative home-rule forces in the state are becoming increasingly aware of the irrevocability of LAFCo decisions (with no administrative or court review). One way in which to mitigate this exercise of "dictatorial" power is to create a two-step review process--as in the case of the typical zoning decision that is made by a planning commission, but can be appealed to a city council or county board of supervisors. On the premise that creation of a state-level board would limit the power of local LAFCos, conservative forces might approve such a measure. A coalition of people holding these two sets of views could form the basis for the majority necessary to pass this beneficial reform.

The Need for Publication

It is clear that LAFCos are not now producing realistic standards in published form, nor are LAFCos recording decisions so that a proponent who wants to determine the "case law" can easily do so. Even the LAFCos that keep the best records only note a few sentences, or perhaps a page, recording the disposition of a given case. These records are seldom indexed or arranged so as to be helpful to one who wishes to discover the types of argument his county's LAFCo is likely to find persuasive, the intricacies of developing policy, and his chances for success. (*The First 500* report in San Bernardino County is a notable exception.)

The publication of well-indexed reports of a state-level review board would be helpful. Such a procedure would not mean that the individual differences between counties would be ignored, or that a uniform state-level set of standards would straitjacket county decision-making. Rather, decisions containing a comprehensive statement of the facts of a particular case, including discussion of the pattern of development unique to the county concerned, would allow continued recognition of regional differences. Indeed, forcing careful thought about the type of development contemplated would lead to more precise differentiation in development patterns.

Another reason for a state-level review board has been touched upon earlier. A single, state-level review board would be able to maintain a staff with greater ability and more developed expertise than is possible for each county, who cannot each maintain a computer programmer, a first-rate economist, an urban designer, and a political scientist.

SOME PROPOSALS FOR FURTHER RESEARCH AND ANALYSIS

As noted in the Preface, this study has sought to provide an introduction to LAFCos: how they began, what they are, how they operate, what their impact has been, and how they may develop in the future. Thus, Chapter II dealt generally with the quantitative impact of LAFCos--the aggregate numbers of various kinds of proposals that LAFCos have handled. While it appeared in almost every case that LAFCos have not greatly affected the actual aggregate results, the impressionistic material in Chapters III and IV implied that LAFCos have had considerable impact. The apparent ambiguity of such findings emphasizes the need for more detailed and extensive analyses of LAFCo performance in California, as well as the experience of other states.

Useful investigations could be made in a number of areas now, while others may be more rewarding in the future. An example of the former would be a study of special districts created before and after the LAFCos, with special attention devoted to (1) budget, (2) location, (3) amount of functional overlap with other governmental entities, and (4) composition of governing bodies. Such information could presumably be entered on computer cards so that changes in patterns of key variables could be examined. Hopefully, such a study would show a shift in the location of new district formations away from urban areas (particularly fringes) and toward rural, desert, or topograhically distinct areas where no alternative method of service is feasible. It might also show a decrease in functional overlaps, an increase in budgets (showing that new districts are substantive rather than "paper" districts), and a shift in the type of governing boards now being elected to new special districts.

It may also now be timely to study rural LAFCos. As indicated earlier, this monograph has focused on LAFCos in urban counties, but a study of rural areas might well ask whether rural LAFCos are preventing the type of crazy-quilt development that, as we have seen, was the pre-LAFCo bane of urban counties. If such a study showed that rural LAFCos have accomplished little, it could be argued either that they should exist only in urban counties, or that several large LAFCo-like entities should be established with jurisdiction over entire metropolitan areas.

        In addition, detailed questionnaires could be sent
to planners, city managers, directors of special districts, developers, and members of various interested
organizations. Answers might reveal useful information
regarding the popularity of LAFCos, and provide some
leads on their political prospects.[9]

        Looking to the future, the following study probably
should be deferred for several years until statistically
significant numbers of incorporations have been subject
to LAFCo review. Select characteristics of pre- and
post-LAFCo city incorporations might be analyzed. The
examination in Chapter II focused on only a few variables,
primarily population and assessed valuation. A study of
many variables--including geographical location, amounts
of industry, various types of potential tax revenue, extent of open space, and racial composition of the
population--could profitably use a computer, and might
reveal significant changes that are not apparent in gross
figures.

        Further, a statewide analysis of the impact of the
District Reorganization Act of 1965 should be conducted
in several years. William Zion has already done a study
of the act's impact in the nine Bay Area counties,[10] but
the act is so complex and so recent that this monograph
has not attempted to determine its full effect.

        Finally, a study of other states' experiences with
municipal incorporations and special district legislation
may be valuable. In this respect, boundary review systems in Alaska, Minnesota, and Wisconsin would be of particular interest. In addition, it would be helpful to
study the experiences of county and regional commissions
analogous to LAFCos that were created in several Oregon
metropolitan areas in 1969. While their functions are
similar to those of LAFCos, their composition is different, and their powers appear to be greater. Thus, as
Oregon commissions gain experience, some revealing comparative case studies could be made between California
and her neighbor to the north.

In short, the systems of other states, along with many other aspects of California's LAFCos, provide a rich research field whose possibilities await exploration.

NOTES

CHAPTER V

1. See particularly State of California, Assembly, Interim Committee Reports (Volume 6, Number 16) Final Report of the Assembly Interim Committee on Municipal and County Government, *Annexation and Related Incorporation Problems in the State of California*, testimony of Lewis Keller, pp. 22-42.

2. "Annexation Act of 1913," *California Government Code*, §35100 - 35180.

3. "Annexation of Uninhabited Territory Act of 1939," *California Government Code*, §35300 - 35326.

4. Julian Community Services District (September 29, 1964), Stewart Canyon Community Services District (November 12, 1964), Borrego Springs Park Community Services District (March 30, 1965), Cardiff Marina Community Services District (June 22, 1965), Canebrake County Water District (August 19, 1965), and Valley Center Community Services District (December 14, 1965).

5. Resolution 10-R-66. November 3, 1966.

6. Letter, October 11, 1967, W. V. Waggoner to James W. Powell.

7. See Chapter II, Note 1. Assuming that most annexations of additional territory to existing special districts, and most uninhabited city annexations would not merit state-level review, and that only 1/4 to 1/3 of other cases would, the percentage of appealable cases approaches five percent.

8. James L. Clark and Louis F. Weschler (Davis: Institute of Governmental Affairs, University of California, August 1965).

9. Such a poll study of various groups was made in San Diego County by two students at San Diego State College, Joe Henry Hall and Charles Cardillo, Jr. The results were included in a seminar paper presented to Dr. Richard W. Bigger: "Local Agency Formation Commission: Action and Reaction in San Diego County." Similar studies are now underway in Santa Barbara under a grant from the American Society for Public Administration.

10. The major findings are tabulated on page 57.

APPENDICES

APPENDIX I

CALIFORNIA CITIES INCORPORATED BETWEEN JANUARY 1, 1955 and SEPTEMBER 20, 1963

City	Year	County	Population	Assessed Valuation	Per Capita Assessed Valuation
Cabazon	1955	Riverside	885	$ 650,290	$ 760
Cupertino	1955	Santa Clara	1,752	3,747,360	1,567
Dairyland	1955	Orange	550	1,746,770	3,175
Newark	1955	Alameda	6,948	12,993,750	1,872
Anderson	1956	Shasta	4,246	3,407,760	811
Baldwin Park	1956	Los Angeles	32,334	25,407,760	794
Fremont	1956	Alameda	26,778	48,193,970	1,853
Los Altos Hills	1956	Santa Clara	3,138	7,493,690	2,417
Bellflower	1957	Los Angeles	35,000	41,573,570	1,187
Bradbury	1957	Los Angeles	810	1,996,760	246
Duarte	1957	Los Angeles	10,000	10,258,350	1,025
Escalon	1957	San Joaquin	2,100	2,414,580	804
Fountain Valley	1957	Orange	597	2,607,350	4,367
Industry	1957	Los Angeles	625	18,888,680	30,223
Irwindale	1957	Los Angeles	700	9,962,870	2,465
McFarland	1957	Kern	2,500	1,476,260	590
Monte Sereno	1957	Santa Clara	2,343	2,371,430	1,013
Norwalk	1957	Los Angeles	59,500	58,077,080	967
Pacifica	1957	San Mateo	21,000	14,019,005	667

APPENDIX I (cont'd)

City	Year	County	Population	Assessed Valuation	Per Capita Assessed Valuation
Rolling Hills Estates	1957	Los Angeles	4,000	$ 5,429,150	$ 1,357
Santa Fe Springs	1957	Los Angeles	11,200	47,828,690	4,271
Westminster	1957	Orange	10,755	14,745,420	1,365
Artesia	1959	Los Angeles	9,500	9,191,930	967
Del Mar	1959	San Diego	1,000	8,165,400	8,165
Grover City	1959	San Luis Obispo	2,750	4,741,010	1,724
Half Moon Bay	1959	San Mateo	1,175	2,378,583	201
Lawndale	1959	Los Angeles	28,000	15,490,770	553
Rosemead	1959	Los Angeles	18,000	15,175,840	842
Arvin	1960	Kern	5,000	2,516,870	503
Commerce	1960	Los Angeles	8,300	172,495,520	20,782
Cudahy	1960	Los Angeles	2,500	8,455,265	3,382
Farmersville	1960	Tulare	1,300	1,434,920	1,103
Novato	1960	Marin	25,000	14,893,190	599
San Dimas	1960	Los Angeles	8,000	9,180,340	1,147
Bell Gardens	1961	Los Angeles	26,000	18,833,430	724
Brisbane	1961	San Mateo	4,500	2,973,240	660
Hidden Hills	1961	Los Angeles	1,650	3,335,910	2,018
Pleasant Hill	1961	Contra Costa	26,000	20,917,910	804
Weed	1961	Siskiyou	3,500	2,243,045	640
Villa Park	1962	Orange	1,446	2,358,040	1,637

Palmdale	1962	Los Angeles	8,000	9,793,200	1,224
Rohnert Park	1962	Sonoma	3,000	3,800,400	1,266
Victorville	1962	San Bernardino	7,200	10,572,120	1,468
Cotati	1963	Sonoma	1,434	1,523,780	1,088
San Marcos	1963	San Diego	3,200	7,014,910	2,192
Vista	1963	San Diego	20,000	24,418,310	1,220

All information is from California, Office of the Controller, *Annual Report of Financial Transactions Concerning Cities in California* from fiscal years 1954-55 to 1962-63.

The population column represents estimates at time of incorporation.

The figures on assessed valuation are taken from the first fiscal year in which they are reported (usually the year after incorporation).

Per capita assessed valuation is derived from the two preceding columns.

APPENDIX II

CALIFORNIA CITIES INCORPORATED AFTER SEPTEMBER 20, 1963
BUT INITIATED EARLIER AND NOT REVIEWED BY LAFCOS

City	Year	County	Population	Assessed Valuation	Per Capita Assessed Valuation
Desert Hot Springs	1963	Riverside	2,979	$ 9,223,600	$ 3,095
Ridgecrest	1963	Kern	6,400	6,568,160	1,026
Clayton	1964	Contra Costa	1,075	1,428,180	1,335
Hawaiian Gardens	1964	Los Angeles	3,300	5,901,630	1,787
Norco	1964	Riverside	10,000	-	-
Camarillo	1964	Ventura	13,500	22,690,570	1,680
Thousand Oaks	1964	Ventura	22,000	47,658,670	2,166
Morro Bay	1964	San Luis Obispo	7,700	47,093,510	6,166
Portola Valley	1964	San Mateo	3,500	14,152,940	4,043

All figures are from Controller's reports, cited above, for 1963 and 1964.

SELECTED READINGS

The bulk of the material used for this monograph consists of memos, letters, reports, maps, studies, hearing reports, and personal interviews. All of the documents I have collected have been placed in the Library of the Institute of Governmental Studies at the University of California, Berkeley.

Glennon, William E. "New Control over Municipal Formation and Annexation." IV *Santa Clara Lawyer* 125-135 (1963-64). Contains a valuable report of the legislative history of LAFCos.

Goldbach, John. "Local Formation Commissions: CCalifornia's Struggle over Municipal Incorporations." *Public Administration Review*, 25 (3): 213-220 (September 1965). Presents a brief overview of the institution.

_____. "Boundary Change in California: The Local Agency Formation Commissions." To be published by the Institute of Governmental Affairs, University of California, Davis. A comprehensive study of LAFCos.

Intergovernmental Council on Urban Growth. *Report on a Statewide Survey of Local Agency Formation Commissions 1966* (Sacramento: 1966). This report is an excellent summary of LAFCo activities through 1966, and is currently the definitive study of LAFCos.

Rigney, Robert B. *Opportunities, Problems and Landmark Decisions of the San Bernardino County Local Agency Formation Commission* (San Bernardino County: April 28, 1966). A description of the more interesting work of the San Bernardino LAFCo.

San Bernardino County Local Agency Formation Commission. *The First 500*, by Robert B. Rigney (January

1968). A careful study of the first 500 decisions by
the county's LAFCo, prepared by one of the most thought-
ful of the LAFCo executive officers.

Scott, Stanley, Lewis Keller and John C. Bollens.
*Local Governmental Boundaries and Areas: New Policies
for California* (Berkeley: University of California,
Bureau of Public Administration, February 1961). 1961
Legislative Problems Series, No. 2. The seminal academ-
ic work which led to the formation of LAFCos.

State of California. Assembly. Interim Committee
Reports 1959-1961. Volume 6, No. 16. Final Report of
the Assembly Interim Committee on Municipal and County
Government. *Annexation and Related Incorporation Problems in the State of California.* An important document
summarizing the positions of concerned groups with respect to LAFCos.

_____. _____. Interim Committee Reports 1963-1965.
Volume 6, No. 22. Final Report of the Assembly Interim
Committee on Municipal and County Government. *(3) Operations of the Local Agency Formation Commissions.* A useful study of the operations of LAFCos to September 30,
1964.

Zion, William. Untitled study of the impact of
Local Agency Formation Commissions on special districts
in the San Francisco Bay Area. (Publication pending)
This is the best study of the impact of the District Reorganization Act on special districts, as administered
by LAFCos.